LOVE

OUR JOY

This book is a guide
for evangelization,
for spiritual growth of the true Christian,
and for grounding believers in the Word of God.

OUR JOY

best baby

all smiles

mommy's boy

this book belongs to:
Kimberly
E.
Perez
&
Genesis
Novillo

daddy's little man

cherished moment

Becoming A Christian

Myron L. Philippi

Faithful Life Publishers
Lebanon, Pennsylvania

FIRST PRINTING in Spanish, December 1995
2,000 copies

SECOND REVISION in Spanish, March 1997
3,000 copies

THIRD REVISION in Spanish, April 2001
4,000 copies

FOURTH REVISION in Spanish, May 2003
10,000 copies

*****

FIRST PRINTING in English, October 1997
4,000 copies

SECOND REVISION in English, January 2005
4,000 copies

THIRD REVISION in English, January 2007
6,000 copies

To order more copies or receive spiritual help, contact:
Myron L. Philippi
6465 99ᵗʰ Way North #17B
Saint Petersburg, Florida 33708
Tel. 1-727-393-7846
E-Mail: philippi@becoming-a-christian.org
Website: www.becoming-a-christian.org
        or
Myron L. Philippi
%Baptist World Mission
P.O. Box 1246
Decatur, AL 35602
Tel. 256-353-2221
*****

ISBN 0-9727648-1-X

Published by Faithful Life Publishers
Lebanon, PA 17046

Cover artwork and book drawings: D.G. Jose Orozco Rodriguez, Tel: (011) 52-333-344-0923
Guadalajara, Jalisco, MX

Scripture quotations are from the Authorized King James Version of the Holy Bible.

Printed in the United States
15 14 13 12 11 10 09 08 07   3 4 5 6 7

I dedicate this new revision of Becoming a Christian in the English language to my beloved wife, Dotty F. Philippi. She has been faithful to the Lord, as she has devotedly backed me in the ministry for the past 50 years. We have raised four children, and she has faithfully served in the children and women's ministries on the mission field with me. She has enriched my life, exceeded all expectations, and inspired me to do my best for the Lord.

Myron L. Philippi

Table of Contents

Recommendations
from pastors and missionaries

Becoming A Christian is a Bible study book, which takes a lost person through a series of studies on sin, repentance, salvation, and basic discipleship. This book was written because of the necessity for adequate material to be put in the hands of Christians to encourage them to begin Bible studies with the unsaved. These are lessons that may be used to ground Christians in the Word of God and to motivate them to be soul winners. This book can also deepen the Christian's awareness of the need for sound doctrine. Learn what it means to really be a Christian through these lessons. Pastor Myron Philippi is a veteran missionary of 49 years, and writes with a Biblical approach to evangelism.

Pastor Gordon Sears
Song Fest • Coldwater, Michigan

Simple, non-threatening and thoroughly biblical are some of the words that come to mind to describe Pastor Myron Philippi's Bible study book, *Becoming A Christian.* Designed primarily as a tool for soul winning and discipleship, this book will give courage and confidence to believers to reach out to the unsaved through one-on-one Bible studies.

Becoming A Christian is a survey of the basic Bible doctrines that every believer should know and understand. Every age group in our church has been able to study this book and many have experienced the joy of having Bible studies with unsaved family and friends. We have had the opportunity to be challenged by Pastor Philippi's fervency for souls and his passion for soul winning. I highly recommend this book that has been used for many souls to come to Christ.

Pastor Travis D. Smith
Hillsdale Baptist Church • Tampa, Florida

Becoming A Christian is simple and easy to use. The approach of this Bible study book makes it less intimidating to share the Gospel of Christ with friends and neighbors. Thoroughly biblical in content, even the young Christian can be confident in conducting a Bible study without fear of knowing what to say. After Brother Philippi presented *Becoming A Christian* to our people, I had several come to me and say, "Pastor, I can do this." I am grateful to Brother Philippi in helping our people share the Gospel by giving them such a valuable tool as this Bible study book.

Pastor K. D. Bodwell
Windsor Baptist Church • Loves Park, Illinois

We use *Becoming a Christian* in our church in Ensenada, Mexico, for Bible studies with both saved and unsaved people. We use the book with the lost, because it presents the Gospel in a thorough, but easy-to-understand manner for all ages. They can really comprehend their lost condition, repent of their sin, and give themselves to the Lord Jesus Christ, so that they can be truly saved. We use the book with the saved, to disciple them, and to be sure that they truly understand the Christian life. I strongly recommend *Becoming a Christian* for home Bible studies to be promoted in all churches.

Pastor Donald Holmes

Missionary, Baptist World Mission • Ensenada, Baja California, Norte

We thank God for the discipleship training that is ongoing and for the new Bible studies that have been started. We are using Myron Philippi's *Llegando A Ser Cristiano (Becoming a Christian)* in these Bible studies. It is an evangelistic tool to get people interested in the Bible and to teach them God's plan of salvation. It has been an effective tool in Hermosillo, Mexico, and it is our prayer that it will have the same effectiveness everywhere we minister.

Pastor Shawn Clapp

Missionary, International Baptist Missions • Tempe, Arizona

Foreword

Myron Philippi is a veteran missionary of 49 years. He first served in Venezuela for 14 years. Upon returning from Venezuela, he began a work among the Spanish-speaking people of Indianapolis, Indiana, which he pastored for nine years. In 1978 Baptist World Mission appointed him for service in Guadalajara, Mexico. In 1980 Brother Philippi, along with his wife, Dotty, began their ministry in rented facilities in Guadalajara. Later the church bought land in an expanding part of the city, remodeled the old horse barn on the property, and met there. Now the church has built a beautiful 750-seat auditorium, along with educational space, on that land. This thriving church currently averages about 300 in attendance. They are now reaching out and starting other churches in metropolitan Guadalajara.

One reason for God's blessing on the work in Guadalajara is Brother Philippi's fervent, sane, biblical approach to evangelism. He has written a Bible study book, which takes a lost person through a series of studies on sin, repentance, salvation, and basic discipleship. At any given time, the families in his church are conducting thirty-five to forty sessions with lost people each week. Brother Philippi's method accomplishes several things:

1. It involves the church members in regular, consistent personal evangelism.

2. It gives a clear, thorough Gospel presentation.

3. It starts the new believer in basic discipleship.

This book is the English translation from the Spanish of the Bible study, *Llegando A Ser Cristiano*. It is solidly biblical in its presentation. It has been tested and proven in the laboratory of missionary church-planting experience. I am happy to recommend it. May God use it for His glory in the English-speaking world as He has used it in Latin America.

Dr. Fred Moritz
Executive Director, Baptist World Mission • Decatur, Alabama

Preface

This book was written because of the great necessity for adequate material to put in the hands of Christians to encourage them to begin Bible studies with the unsaved. It is a helpful Scriptural guide they can use to show others how to become a Christian and be truly transformed by the grace of God. In our church in Guadalajara, Mexico, even new Christians enthusiastically accept the challenge to hold a one-on-one Bible class and share what they have learned, using this book. Our prayer is that God may use these lessons to ground Christians in the Word of God and motivate them to be soul winners. This book can also help deepen the Christian's awareness of the need for sound doctrine.

A farmer is a steward of the ground. He is responsible to be careful so that it will produce in the future. Likewise, pastors and teachers of the Gospel are also stewards of the *ground* where the Word of God is sown. We all are responsible to the Lord Jesus Christ for what we do in preparing the *ground* so that it will produce true spiritual fruit in the future. The Word of God needs to be carefully planted in the hearts of individuals so that they will understand. "Thou therefore, my son, be strong in the grace that is in Christ Jesus. And the things that thou hast heard of me among many witnesses, the same commit thou to faithful men, who shall be able to teach others also." (2 Timothy 2:1–2)

We give thanks to God for the ideas and suggestions that have come to me through pastors, missionaries, and teachers of the Word of God. Their suggestions have made it possible to place a more complete book in your hands and to enable you to teach others also.

Myron L. Philippi

Welcome, Student

We greet you in the name of our Lord and Savior Jesus Christ. We are thankful that you are taking time to study God's Word. We want to encourage you to make this a priority in your life as you study the lessons faithfully and fill in the blanks, asking God to guide you and help you understand His Word as you look up every Scripture.

Study carefully and be diligent. Do not let other things crowd out your desire to study God's Word. We all need to come to Christ Jesus for He is the only "way, the truth and the life." (John 14:6) The way of salvation is clearly presented in the Word of God in order that we might truly be born again by the Spirit of God and receive His true salvation.

In Matthew 7:13, Christ Jesus contrasts two ways and two destinies; one way leads to life, and the other leads to eternal destruction. This is a clear warning that God gives to us, and we must make a choice. This is the most important decision of your life. God desires to bring you into a wonderful personal relationship with Himself through His Son, Christ Jesus. It is our sincere desire that He will become your personal Savior.

"But these are written, that ye might believe that Jesus is the Christ, the Son of God; and that believing ye might have life through His name." (John 20:31)

May God richly bless you as you study His Word.

Myron L. Philippi

— Chapter 1—

The True Christian

Therefore if any man be in Christ, he is a new creature:
old things are passed away; behold, all things are become new.
2 Corinthians 5:17

What is a true Christian?

Many wrong ideas exist concerning who is really a Christian. It is imperative
to understand how to be saved according to the Word of God. Romans 10:17
says, "So then faith cometh by hearing, and hearing by the message
of God." The plan of God for salvation is perfect (complete), not an incomplete design made by men.

As a good cook always checks to make sure that she has not forgotten any
ingredient in the recipe, even so we should take more care and concern in
understanding God's plan of salvation as presented in His Word. It is clearly
given with accuracy in the Bible and there should be no doubt as to what God
plainly teaches us. We need to be sure that we follow with care the instructions
that God gives to us. True salvation, which is of God, does not come by doing
good works, by making great personal sacrifices, by fulfilling certain moral
duties, rites, or laws, nor by being educated or rich. It is only through the grace
of God that we can become a "new creation" in Christ Jesus.

I. The First Christians

1. Besides being called "disciples," by what name were the followers of Jesus Christ first known? (Read Acts 9:2; 19:9,23; 24:14)
   Please underline the correct answer.

   Believers   *Those of the Way,*   or   *Christians*

1

Jesus Christ said in John 14:6, *I am the* __light__ *, the truth, and the life: no man cometh unto the Father, but by me.*

2. In what location were the followers of Jesus Christ first called *Christians*? (Acts 11:25–26) __to Antioch__ . The name *Christian* means – *ones of Christ or the followers of Christ*. It is a direct personal identification with the Lord Jesus Christ.

II. Those who appear to be Christians

Read carefully Matthew 7:21–23. Many teach and preach in the name of God and of Jesus Christ. Is this proof that they truly represent God? __No__

1. Note three things these people had apparently done in the name of Jesus Christ.

   a. __wants to go to heaven__

   b. __that with the name of the Lord they can__ do miracles

   c. __they ~~prasint~~ ~~the~~ appart from god.__

2. Because they used the name of Jesus saying, "Lord, Lord," did these people consider themselves to be Christians? __Supposibly__

3. Do you believe that they were true Christians? __NO__ Why? (Consider Matthew 7:20) __the used the name of god in vain__

4. What were *the people, mentioned in Matthew 7:21–23,* relying on to be able to enter heaven?
   *Place a circle around the letter that best describes what **they** believed.*

   a. They had trusted only in Jesus Christ as their Savior, having repented of their sins with all their heart and giving themselves to Him.

   (b.) They relied on certain accomplishments and works that they had done in order to be saved.

   c. They trusted in their religion, because they felt that it was the best, and it was what their parents had taught them.

5. If a person has the power to prophesy (preach) or even predict the future, cast out demons, or do miracles in the name of Jesus Christ, is this proof that he is a true Christian and that he really belongs to God? __No__ Why? __God could only do that.__

6. Since they did not do these things in the power of God, with what power or authority did they do these things? _Satan_

7. Who can enter into heaven, according to Matthew 7:21? _The ones that believe in god._

8. Read carefully Acts 8:5–25. Simon had believed, and was baptized. Was Simon really a Christian? _Yes_ Had he truly been converted to Jesus Christ? _I don't know_

III. Saul's life before his conversion

The Bible describes the conversion of an unusual man, Saul of Tarsus, who was known by all Jews. Before his conversion he was one of the pharisaical leaders in Judaism and a member of the most important religious organization in that day, the Great Sanhedrin. Read carefully the history of this renown man in Acts 26:9–12 and Philippians 3:4–6.

1. What type of a person was Saul before his conversion? (Acts 9:1) _he was one of the pharisaical leaders in Judaism. He followed the Christians_

2. Before his conversion, Saul felt that there was nothing lacking in his religious life. He tells us in Philippians 3:6, "Concerning zeal, persecuting the church; touching the righteousness which is in the law, _faultless_"

3. What religion did Saul profess? (Galatians 1:13) _none_

4. Did Saul believe in God? _No_ (Acts 22:3) How did he believe? _Because of ignorence and cruelty_

5. What motivated Saul to persecute the followers of Jesus Christ? Read Acts 26:4–12. _He thought this_ Why did Saul believe that it was his responsibility to persecute the Christians? _Because of ignorence and cruelty_

6. Was he fanatical or lukewarm in his fervor to uphold his religious beliefs? (Acts 22:3–4) _He was an_

7. From what we read in Galatians 1:13–14, how do you know that he was fanatical? _for being more jealous than his fathers._

8. Was Saul faithful to his religion? _Si, he taught he was good with god._

3

9. Was Saul confident of what he believed? _Yes_

10. In what was Saul trusting? (Philippians 3:4–6) _Yes_ In this passage, what does the word "flesh" mean? _Believing in himself._

11. Did Saul have a personal relationship with God before his conversion or was he just a religious man? (1 Timothy 1:13) _n He only Trusted in himself._

12. According to the Word of God, what was lacking in Saul's life? _Believing in God_

13. Can a person believe in God, be fervent in his religion, be very sincere and convinced that he is in the truth, and at the same time be very wrong and not be a true Christian? _Yes_

IV. The conversion of Saul _Mon. March 10, 2008_
Read the personal testimony of Saul in Acts 22:3–16, and also in Acts 9:1–22, to understand how his conversion occurred.

1. What did Saul see from heaven? _A thunder of light_

2. What was his reaction? _He fell from fear of God_

3. What did Saul hear? _He heard God's voice_

4. Who spoke with Saul? (Acts 9:5) _Jesus of Nazareth_

5. Where did Saul go after he saw the light and heard the voice of Jesus Christ? _He went to Damascus_

6. How many days was Saul blind? _For 3 days_

7. How many days was Saul fasting because of his sadness for his sinful condition? _3 days_

8. How do we know that Saul was truly converted and that it was not just a desire to unite with a new sect or religion? (Acts 9:20) _because he preached Christ in the synagogues._

9. How was Saul convinced that Jesus Christ was God and not just a common person? (Acts 9:5, 20; 26:15; Romans 1:3–4) _He himself said, he was the son of God_

10. Today, how can we be convinced of the fact that Jesus Christ is God? (Mark 14:60–64) _That he will sit in his throne_

4

11. What are the results of a true conversion that we have seen in this lesson? (2 Corinthians 5:17) (NAS) *people* *creatures* *hearts* *spirits* *sons of god*.

Study carefully the passage regarding the conversion of Saul in Acts 9:17–19. In a few brief words we are told of Saul's meeting with Ananias, and the message God had for Saul. We see that Saul believed, obeyed and was baptized in water by Ananias. Now read Acts 22:12–16 where there is more information regarding Saul's conversion. Ananias, the servant of the Lord, gave Saul the Gospel message and Saul believed. When the Apostle Paul gave his testimony before King Agrippa regarding his conversion, he told the king what Ananias had said: "now why tarriest thou? arise, and be *baptized*."

The word *baptism* is mentioned several places in the Bible, however, not all refer to water baptism. The word *baptism* in Greek means – *put into or place into* something or someone. In this reference there is no mention of water, but Ananias tells Saul to place himself in or place all his confidence in the Lord Jesus Christ as his personal Savior. It happened when he truly repented of his sin and gave himself to the Lord Jesus Christ with all his heart.

Ananias continued saying in verse 16, "and wash away thy sins, calling on the name of the Lord." Saul called upon the Lord Jesus Christ for salvation and his sins were washed away. The only way that a person can have his sins washed away is through the redeeming work of the Lord Jesus Christ when on the cross of Calvary He took upon Himself our sin and died for us receiving our punishment. Saul repented of his sin, and put his complete faith and confidence in the Lord Jesus Christ as his Savior by calling upon Him for forgiveness. Saul did call upon the Lord Jesus Christ in prayer and was converted. God forgave Saul's sin, and now his greatest desire was to serve Him.

Regrettably, many desire to see lights, hear voices, or have some spectacular experience in order to have a conversion like Saul's. The method that God used with Saul was appropriate for his need; however, God uses many different things to get our attention and bring us to faith in Christ Jesus. God's plan or method of salvation never changes. It is always the same. You must not ignore the fact that the Lord Jesus Christ wants you to be converted to Him. Do you realize this? *Yes*

1. Did the light give Saul his salvation? _NO_

2. Did the words that Jesus spoke to Saul give him salvation? (Acts 9:4-6)
   _NO_

3. Did his sadness through fasting save him? _NO_

4. What command did Jesus give to Saul in Acts 9:6? _Arive and_
   go into the city, and it shall be told thee
   what thou must do.

5. Was Saul converted on the way to Damascus or with Ananias? _with_
   What brought you to that conclusion? _Because Ananias_
   told him about Jesus
   The answer is very obvious regarding Saul's conversion. Ananias gave
   the Gospel message to Saul and he understood, repented of his sin,
   trusted Christ Jesus as his personal Savior, and was converted giving
   himself to the Lord Jesus Christ. Paul's life and very being became the
   property of God.

   Mon 4/7/08

V. The life of Saul after his conversion

Study in Acts 26:16–20, the commission that Christ gave to Saul. Jesus
Christ gave him the order to go to the gentiles and preach the message of
salvation.

1. In what way was Saul changed after his conversion? (verse 20) _I_
   preached that they should repent and
   turn to God and prove their repentance in their

2. To what people was Saul sent? _the gentiles_ The name, *gentiles,* is
   mentioned in verse 17, and is making reference to everyone who is not
   of the Jewish race.

3. In Acts 26:18, Christ demands that the unsaved "turn from _darkne_
   _ss_ to _light_ , and from the power of _Satan_ unto God, that they
   may receive forgiveness of _sins_ , and inheritance among
   them which are sanctified (the saved) by faith that is in me."

4. According to Acts 3:19, how can you receive forgiveness of your sins?
   Repent and then turn

5. According to 2 Corinthians 5:17, what are some of the results of a true
   conversion? _We are new people/creatures_
   Please mention several new things that had taken place in the life of
   Saul: _saved, baptized, preached, loyal_

6

VI. What is a true Christian?

Read the following verses and circle the numbers which best describe a true Christian: Acts 4:11–12; John 3:3; John 8:31–32, 1 Peter 1:22–23.

1. A true Christian is a person that believes in God with all his heart. This means that this person has placed (deposited) all his confidence in the redeeming work that the Lord Jesus Christ did on the cross for him by dying for his sins.

2. A true Christian is one who has studied the Bible under the direction of excellent religious teachers.

3. A true Christian is one who believes in God and tries to do the best that he can by doing a lot of good works in order to gain his salvation.

4. A true Christian is one who was born into a Christian family, is baptized, and faithfully follows the traditions of the church.

5. A true Christian is one that recognizes his terrible sinful condition and has repented of his sin and with all of his heart given himself to the Lord Jesus Christ in order to be forgiven.

6. A true Christian is one who has repented of sin that he has committed, trusting Christ Jesus as his Savior, therefore has been born again into the family of God. This is not a physical birth, but a spiritual one. As true evidence of this salvation there is a transformation in his life.

REVIEW QUESTIONS
Chapter 1: The true Christian

Mon. 4/28/08

1. To become a Christian is it sufficient to have a religion, and have faith in God? __NO__ Why? _Because the religion doesn't save us._

2. Are all who consider themselves to be Christians, really saved? _NO_ Why? _Because not all people are saved_

3. Is it proof that a person belongs to Christ if he preaches, casts out demons, and does miracles and wonderful things in name of Jesus Christ? _NO_

Why? They dont have powers to do all these things. / thay do it with the power of satan.

4. If you believe in God, are you assured of a place in heaven? (James 2:19) _NO_ Why? because even the demons believe in hime.

5. If you are faithful to your religion and sincerely and fervently believe in it, will this save you? _NO_ Why? (Galatians 2:16) because # we are saved by the faith and for grace.

6. Is it possible for you to have the assurance of going to heaven when you die, even while you are still living? _Si_ How? his shedding blood, repentance, aceeptance.

7. Are only those saved who have repented of their sins, trusted <u>only</u> in Jesus Christ as their personal Savior, and given themselves to Him with all their heart? _Yes_ Why? I accepted him in my heart.

8. Can a person become a Christian by doing good works? _NO_ Why? (Ephesians 2:8–9) Even doing good we are sinners.

9. Can people gain heaven through their generosity, giving their possessions and money to the needy? _NO_ Why? you cant buy salvation.

10. Can you be a Christian by being a faithful church member? _NO_ Why? church doesn't save you.

11. Is a person saved by being baptized in water? _NO_ Why? its just a symbolism of salvation

12. If a person does good works in the name of Jesus Christ, does it indicate that he is a true Christian? _NO_ Why? he's using Jesus's name in vain

13. Does our own personal faith save us? _yes_ Why? (Galatians 2:16; Romans 10:17; Ephesians 2:8–9) _We are saved through_ _but not by works._

14. Is it true that all religions lead us to God? _no_ Why? (John 14:6) _Because Jesus is the only way to God._

15. Is it sufficient to be sincere in your religion in order to achieve salvation? _no_ Why? _We should also believe._

16. Was Saul well-educated and prepared in his religion? _yes_ How do you know? _Because he himself said that he was good into his religion._

17. Did Saul love, and help the Christians before his conversion to Jesus Christ? _No_ Why? _It says in the Bible that he followed the Christians to make them suffer._

18. Did Saul believe in God before his conversion? _yes_ How do you know? _Because it was the religion of his fathers._

19. Could Saul's fervent belief in God before his conversion, save him from eternal condemnation? _No_ Why? _Because he still followed the Christians._

20. Was Saul saved from eternal condemnation as a result of his conversion to Jesus Christ? _Yes_ How do you know? _God gave him another chance._

21. Saul saw a bright light and heard the voice of God. Did that experience save him? _yes_ How do you know? _Because God made him blind._

22. If you have an extraordinary experience in your life, is that proof that you are saved? _No_ How do you know? _Anyone can be saved. its not necessary to be a really bad person._

9

23. If you believe that Jesus Christ is God, does that belief save you? _Yes_
    Why? _Cause God (Jesus) gives you eternal life._

24. If a person's life drastically changes, is that proof of a true conversion to
    Jesus Christ? _Yes_ Why? _Not all ~~the~~ peoples life have to change completely._

25. Just because there has been a change or reformation in an individual's life,
    does this indicate that he is of God? _Yes_ Why? _A person has to change in order to follow Jesus._

• Please memorize 2 Corinthians 5:17 and explain it in your own words. _We don't follow anyone like a Pope to guide us. Even though that person told us about Jesus . . ._

• Do you feel that your personal life is pleasing to God? _Yes._

• Is your life in harmony with God? _Yes._

• Do you know for sure that you are a "new creation" in Jesus Christ? _Yes._

Note: If you do not have a person to help you study these lessons, please send
   your answers to the review questions and any doubts that you might
   have regarding this lesson to the Bible Institute Correspondence Department: philippi@becoming-a-christian.org

If you prefer you may send your letter by U.S. Postal Service to:

Pastor Myron L. Philippi
P.O. Box 1246
Decatur, AL 35602

— Chapter Two —

The Universal Problem: Sin

For all have sinned, and come short of the glory of God.

Romans 3:23

The Perfect Creation of God

The Word of God speaks little about *eternity past*. We do know that God is eternal and in *eternity past* He created the angels first. Later, God created the world, everything visible and invisible, in six days. (Genesis 1–2) Even though there is no proof that supports their theories, many deny or ignore the fact that the universe, and everything in it, was created by all-mighty God. Although some do not believe God's Word, they still are responsible to give an account of their deeds before Him on Judgment Day. God declares in Hebrews 9:27, "it is appointed unto men once to die, but after this the judgment." With this declaration, it is fitting to say that the God of the Bible is completely in charge. The theories, including evolution, which deny God's existence, work, and purposes for all mankind, are tremendous lies that have their origin in Satan.

When Job, a true follower of God, desired to show his own wisdom, God responded in Job 38:1–7 with many questions about the creation of the world, and asked him about *eternity past*, saying, "Who is this that darkeneth counsel by words without knowledge? Gird up now thy loins like a man; for I will demand of thee, and answer thou me. Where wast thou when I laid the foundations of the earth? declare, if thou hast understanding. Who hath laid the measures thereof, if thou knowest? or who hath stretched the line upon it? Whereupon are the _foundations_ thereof fastened? or who laid the corner stone thereof; When the morning stars sang together, and all the sons of God (the angels) shouted for joy?"

I. When did the first sin occur?

Ezekiel 28:11–19 explains how the angel Lucifer sinned against God. In verse 17 it says: "Thine heart was lifted up because of thy _beauty_, thou hast corrupted thy wisdom by reason of thy _splendor_ : I will cast thee to the ground, I will lay thee before kings, that they may behold thee." Sin did not exist before Lucifer sinned and became Satan. Because of his vanity, vainglory, pride, greed and jealousy, the angel Lucifer rebelled against God, therefore committing the first sin. The sin of Lucifer took place when he placed his own will over the will of God, desiring to be equal to God.

II. How did sin enter into the world?

Sin entered into the human race by means of deception and disobedience, motivated by disbelief. Eve, upon listening to the voice of Satan, was tempted, fell into his trap of deceit, and ate the prohibited fruit. Adam ate of the same fruit, knowing that his wife had disobeyed God. This is explained in 1 Timothy 2:14, stating, "Adam was not _deceived_, but the woman being _deceived_ was in the _transgression_." Adam did not want to abandon his wife, Eve. He understood completely what he was doing and also sinned, participating in that which God had prohibited.

1. Did Adam and Eve clearly understand that they had disobeyed God? (Genesis 3:7) _Yes_

2. Did Adam and Eve realize that they had lost the glory of God, which had clothed them? _Yes_

3. What did they do to try to hide their nakedness? _they sewed fig leaves together and made themselves coverings._

4. Did Adam and Eve try to cover up the evidence of their sin because they were ashamed? _Yes_

5. Was it sufficient what they tried to do to repair their sinful condition? _No_

Adam and Eve did a terrible thing by disobeying God. Their own preparations and work were not sufficient to correct the wrong they had done. With all that they did they could not get rid of their sin; they could only cover the visible evidence, which was accusing their conscience. It was not possible through their efforts to have communion once again with God, nor could it bring contentment and peace to their hearts. Both Adam and Eve were sincere, but their sincerity was not sufficient to correct their sinful condition. Why? _Because of their guilt of not doing God's will._

We read in Genesis 3:8–10, that God came to the Garden of Eden to visit Adam and Eve. When they heard His voice, what were they trying to do? _Hide._ Fearfully, Adam and Eve tried to hide from the presence of God! Their efforts to hide the evidence of their sin had failed and something far better was necessary. They had done their very best, but their best was not sufficient to satisfy God's justice. The perfect provision had to come from God, and He was ready to provide it. We have the short story of what God did, described in Genesis 3:21: "Unto Adam also and to his wife did the LORD God make _tunics_ of skins, and _clothed_ them." God had to sacrifice animals as a provision in order to cover their sin. God gave the promise later on that the *Lamb of God*, the Lord Jesus Christ, would come to this world to be sacrificed to pay for all of our sins.

The Apostle Paul explained in Romans 5:12, "Wherefore, as by one man _sinned_ entered into the world, and _death_ by sin; and so death passed upon all _men_, for that _all_ have sinned." We must understand that sin not only had its roots in Adam and Eve, but also has entered our hearts at conception and has corrupted our life since birth. Sin always turns us away from God. All human beings are sinners because of the original sin of disobedience. This sinful nature continues to be passed on from father to children, subsequently to everyone who comes into this world. The reason we sin is because **we are sinners** when we are born into this world. Never can we become sinners because we commit our first sin. **We sin, because we are sinners**. It is very important that we have this clear.

III. What is sin?

1. **"Missing the mark"** is sin. The word "sin" in the ancient Greek, the original language of the New Testament, means – "missing the bulls-eye

13

on the target." All human beings are guilty of having sinned. We cannot reach the mark of perfection and holiness that God requires. Romans 3:10 affirms, "There are none righteous, no, not _one_." Romans 3: 23 says, "For _all_ have sinned, and come _short_ of the glory of God."

2. **The infraction or transgression of God's Law is sin.** God declares in 1 John 3:4, that "whosoever committeth sin transgresseth also the _lawlessness_ for sin is the transgression of the _law_." All transgression of the Law of God is sin. Possible exceptions exist regarding human laws, but no one can be exempt from God's Law.

3. **All injustice is sin.** 1 John 5:17 declares that "All _unrighteous ness_ is sin." The word "just" signifies "right or correct." Injustice is "unfairness or wrong." Proverbs 17:15 declares, "He that justifieth the _wicked_ , and he that condemneth the _unrighteous_ even they both are abomination (great hatred) to the Lord."

4. **Deceitfulness is sin.** When the truth is twisted it is sin. The Apostle Paul warns in Romans 1:18, "the _wrath_ of God is revealed from heaven against all _ungodliness_ and _unrighteousness_ of men, who hold (hold back) the _truth_ in unrighteousness." To "hold back" is the same thing as to twist the truth. 2 Peter 3:16 teaches us that men who are "unlearned and unstable _distort_ (distort)" the Word of God. This is well illustrated in Isaiah 5:20: "Woe unto them that call _evil_ good, and good _evil_; that put darkness for _light_, and light for _darkness_; that put bitter for sweet, and sweet for bitter!" (The word "woe," in this case signifies the judgment or condemnation of God.)

5. **Rebellion against God is sin.** Rebellion against God and His Word brings terrible consequences. God declares in 1 Samuel 15:23, "For _rebellion_ is as the sin of witchcraft, and _insubordination_ is as iniquity and idolatry." We should not take this sin lightly for God considers rebellion to be a terrible offense against Him. Joshua 1:18 gives the warning, "Whosoever he be that doth _rebels_ against thy commandment, and will not hearken unto thy words in all that thou commandest of him, he shall be put to _death_: only be strong and of a good courage." God requires obedience and hates rebellion.

6. **Disobedience is sin.** The sin of disobedience is related to the sin of rebellion. Disobeying God is to rebel against Him. 1 Timothy 1:9–10 teaches: "Knowing this, that the law is not made for a righteous man, but for the lawless and rebellious, for the ungodly and for sinners, for unholy and profane, for murderers of fathers and murderers of mothers, for manslayers, for whoremongers, for them that defile themselves with mankind, for mensteelers, for liars, for perjured persons, and if there be any other thing that is contrary to sound doctrine." God's Word declares that they love their sin and have unrestrained lives. Practicing sin is a deliberate decision. Ephesians 2:2 shows what a person was before giving himself to the Lord. "Wherein in time formerly ye walked according to the course of this world, according to the prince of the power of the air, the spirit that now worketh in the children of disobedience." If we are disobedient to what God requires, it is sin.

7. **Unbelief is sin.** 1 John 5:10 says, "He that believes (deposits all his confidence) on the Son of God hath the witness in himself: he that does not God hath made him a liar; because he believeth testimony the record that God gave of His Son." If we do not wholly trust in what God has declared, we are saying that God is a liar. What does God's Word say regarding the end of those who do not believe Him? The answer is found in Revelation 21:8, "But the fearful, and unbelieving, and abominable, and murderers, and whoremongers, and sorcerers, and idolaters, and all liars, shall have their part in the lake which burns with fire and brimstone: which is the second death."

8. **Ungodliness is sin.** A "godly" life is a life faithful to God in all thoughts, attitudes, actions, worship, and devotion. The word "ungodliness" is the exact opposite of God's holiness. Jude 1:15 declares that the Lord is coming "to execute judgement upon all, and to convince that that are ungodly among them of all their ungodly deeds which they have ungodly committed, and of all their hard speeches which ungodly sinners have spoken against him." Proverbs 13:6 affirms: "Righteousness keepeth him that is upright in the way: but wickedness overthroweth the sinner."

9. **All iniquity is sin.** This is any action against the character of God and

against the moral order that God has given to mankind. As the darkness is the absence of light, so is iniquity the absence of the perfect justice of God. Galatians 5:19–21 mentions some of the things that God hates: "Now the works of the flesh are manifest, which are these; _____, fornication, uncleanness (moral distortions), lasciviousness (lust or lewdness), _____, witchcraft, hatred, _____ (a desire to bypass regulations), _____ (ambition to equal or surpass in an evil way), wrath, _____, seditions, heresies, _____ _____, murders, _____, revellings, and such like: of the which I tell you before, as I have also told you in time past, that they which _____ such things shall not inherit the kingdom of God." People are involved in these types of sin because it is part of their sinful nature.

10. **All lying is sin.** Is a "white" lie a sin, or just a mistake? _____ There is no such thing as a "white" lie. All lies will eventually cause harm and are terrible in the sight of God. In John 8:44 Christ Jesus tells where all lies come from. Where are they from?_____ 1 Timothy 4: 2 tells us that some will depart from the faith, "speaking _____ in hypocrisy; having their conscience seared with a hot iron." Many people lie without remorse, because it is part of their nature. This is actually hypocrisy.

11. **Stealing something or even destroying someone's reputation is sin.** Zephaniah 1:9 says, "In the same day also will I _____ all those that leap on the threshold, which fill their masters' houses with violence and deceit." In Zechariah 5:3 we read, "This is the curse that goeth forth over the face of the whole earth: for every one that _____ shall be cut off as on this side according to it." Many thieves escape man's attention, but God sees them and they can never escape God's judgment. Also, when you borrow something and do not return it, that is stealing.

12. **All the filthy and destructive things that come out of the mouth is sin.** In Ephesians 4:29, God orders us to "let no _____ com-munication proceed out of your mouth." Proverbs 4:24–25 orders us to "Put away from thee a froward (uncontrolled) mouth, and _____ lips put far from thee." Proverbs 8:13 declares what we should hate: "The fear of the Lord is to _____ evil: pride, and arrogancy, and the evil way, and the froward mouth, do I _____." We are all

16

responsible before God for each word that leaves our lips. King Solomon declared in Proverbs 10:19, "In the multitude of words there wanteth not _____: but he that _____ his lips is wise."

13. **The lack of fulfilling our obligations is sin.** This sin of omission is committed when we do not fulfill our responsibilities. James 4:17 says, "Therefore to him that _____ to do _____, and doeth it not, to him it is sin." God makes us responsible for the "good" that we do not do! Many are not interested in reading the Bible to know and understand God's will for their lives. This indifference toward God and His Word is sin.

14. **The lack of forgiveness is sin.** Jesus Christ instructs the Apostles in Matthew 6:12–15 to forgive saying, "And forgive us our _____, (sins) as we forgive our debtors (those that have sinned against us). And lead us not into temptation, but deliver us from evil: For thine is the kingdom, and the power, and the glory, for ever. Amen. For if ye forgive men their trespasses, your heavenly Father will also forgive you: But if ye forgive not men their trespasses, neither will your Father forgive your trespasses." If you refuse to forgive a person who has asked for forgiveness, God will not forgive your sins.

IV. We all are sinners

The Pharisees were the most important religious leaders in Israel. Besides interpreting and teaching the law of the Old Testament, they taught their own laws. By their actions they pretended to be very spiritual. The Jews had been enslaved to the oppression of the legalism of the Pharisees. Jesus Christ identified them in Luke 18:9–12 as sinners. It doesn't matter which religion is represented, all their leaders are sinners, because **"all have sinned."**

1. Although the Pharisees were very religious, was this Pharisee's prayer heard by God? _____ To whom was he really praying? _____

2. Was the righteousness (religiosity and good works) of the Pharisees sufficient to gain them entrance into heaven? _____ Why? _____

   _____

3. What concept did the Pharisees have of themselves? _____

   _____

4. Are all religious leaders sinners? _____ Why? _____

_____

The Publicans were despised, dishonest tax collectors. They were Jews, who embezzled their own people, directly in allegiance to the Roman government. They were hated and considered as terrible sinners. In Luke 18:13–14 Christ Jesus identified them for what they were, sinners.

1. Why were the tax collectors so despised?_____

_____

2. In what condition did the publican find himself before God? _____

_____

3. In Luke 5:27–32 we have an account about another publican. Who was Levi? _____

4. What was Levi doing when Jesus called him? _____

_____

5. Why did the Pharisees think it was terrible that Jesus ate with the publicans? _____

6. What concept did the Pharisees have of the publicans?_____

_____

7. In the illustration found in Luke 5:31–32, "the sick" represent the _____, "the doctor" represents the_____ and those who feel "healthy" are like the_____.

8. Can the doctor do anything for a person who does not consider himself sick? _____ Why? _____

_____

9. Can Jesus Christ save someone who does not consider himself a terrible lost sinner?_____Why?_____

_____

10. Why did Jesus Christ come to this world, according to verse 32? _____

_____

11. Just because you realize that you are a terrible sinner, can God save you if you don't repent of your sin? _____

12. Can Jesus Christ save a sinner that is not truly repented for all his sin? _____ Why? _____

_____

13. Can God force you to repent of your sin against your will? _____

14. Luke 19:1–10 tells about another publican who was converted. Are more "bad" people or more "good" people, converted to Christ? _____ Why? _____

15. Who put into the heart of Zacchaeus the curiosity and desire to see Jesus? _____

16. What evidences in the life of Zacchaeus show that he was truly converted? _____

_____

17. Who are you really deceiving if you try to hide the evil that you have committed? Others? _____ God? _____ Yourself? _____

V. There is none righteous before God.
• Read Romans 3:9–10.
1. In the sight of God, who is better, the religious Jew or the pagan gentile? _____

2. Are we better than the Jews? _____

3. How many "just" or "good" people are there according to the Word of God? _____

• Read Romans 5:12 and Romans 3:23–24.

4. How many people have sinned? _____ We know that Jesus Christ is God, and could not have sinned. Is it possible that there has been another person that has lived on this earth who has not sinned? _____ If so, who? _____

5. When sin entered into the world by Adam and Eve, what else happened to man as a result of sin? (Genesis 2:17 and Romans 5:12) _____

6. According to Genesis 5:5, to what type of death is this referring? ___

_____

19

7. Does Ephesians 2:1 speak of physical death or spiritual death? _____

_____

8. Is there something that man can do *by his own power* to change his sinful condition in order to please God? _____ If so, what? _____

9. According to Isaiah 64:6, how does God see our righteousness? "But we are all as an _____ thing, and all our righteousnesses are as _____ rags; and we all do fade as a leaf; and our iniquities, like the wind, have taken us away."

10. Basing your answer on Matthew 5:27–28, answer the following declarations with <u>True</u> or <u>False</u>:

   a. Whether by act or thought, everyone on earth is a sinner. _____

   b. If you are sincere, doing no harm to others, it is really not important what you do or think. _____

   c. We can disobey the commandments of God with our thoughts and our actions. _____

VI. The consequences of sin

1. Sin brings terrible consequences to our life. After the first sin was committed by Adam and Eve in Genesis 3:1–24, God pronounced judgment upon the earth, animals and Satan; then upon Eve with pain in childbirth, upon Adam with hard work, and problems in his life. Sickness, pain, physical and eternal death are also results of sin.

2. Sin causes division between God and us. The prophet declares in Isaiah 59:2: "But your iniquities have _____ between you and your God, and your sins have _____ his face from you, that he will not hear."

3. Sin deceives us. We are taught in 1 John 1:8: "If we say that we have no sin, we _____ ourselves, and the truth is not in us."

4. One of the consequences of sin is sickness. The Apostle Paul even gave a warning to the Christians of Corinth in 1 Corinthians 11:28–30 saying, "But let a man _____ (judge sin commited) himself, and so let him eat of that bread, and drink of that cup. For he that eateth and drinketh unworthily, eateth and drinketh _____ to himself, not discerning the Lord's body. For this cause many are _____ and _____ among you, and many sleep (died)."

20

5. Sin robs us of joy that only God can give. King David expressed his deep feeling of repentance to God in Psalm 51:8–12: "Make me to hear _____ and gladness; that the bones which thou hast broken may rejoice. Hide thy face from my sins, and blot out all mine iniquities. Create in me a clean heart, O God; and _____ a right spirit within me. Cast me not away from thy presence; and take not thy Holy Spirit from me. Restore unto me the _____ of thy salvation; and uphold me with thy free spirit."

6. Sin brings physical and spiritual death. God declared in Ezekiel 18:4, "Behold, all souls are mine; as the soul of the father, so also the soul of the son is mine: the soul that _____, it shall die." Romans 6:23 clearly states, "For the wages of sin is _____."

7. Sin also brings the judgment of God after death. Hebrews 9:27 confirms this judgment: "And as it is appointed unto men once to die, but after this the _____." The Apostle Paul declared in Acts 17:31, "He (God) hath appointed a day, in the which he will judge the world in _____ by that man (Jesus Christ) whom he hath ordained."

8. What is the consequence of this judgment of sin? This punishment, separation from God, is referred to as *eternal death*. How long does this punishment last? _____ Revelation 21:8 states: "But the fearful, and unbelieving, and abominable, and murderers, and whoremongers, and sorcerers, and idolaters, and all liars, shall have their part in the _____ which burneth with fire and brimstone: which is the second death." Sin brings eternal condemnation in the *lake of fire*. Revelation 20:11–15 reveals the process: "And I saw a great _____ _____, and him that sat on it, from whose face the earth and the heaven fled away; and there was found no place for them. And I saw the dead, small and great, stand before God; and the books were opened: and another book was opened, which is the book of life: and the dead were _____ _ out of those things which were written in the books, according to their _____. And the sea gave up the dead which were in it; and death and hell delivered up the dead which were in them: and they were _____ _ every man according to their works. And death and hell were cast into the _____ of _____. This is the second death." (This death is not annihilation, but the condition of the resurrected unsaved who receive their just punishment for all eternity.) "And whosoever was not

found written in the book of life was _____ into the lake of fire."
The true Christian will not be in this judgment, because he will be with
Christ in heaven, because his name is written in the *Book of Life.*

VII. Man tries to justify himself in vain.

1. One of the tendencies of the human race is to justify one's self. In Luke
    16:15, Jesus Christ accused the Pharisees saying, "Ye are they which
    justify yourselves before men; but God _____ your _____: for that
    which is highly esteemed among men is abomination in the sight of
    God."

2. A human tendency is to think that we are very wise. The prophet an-
    nounced in Isaiah 5:21, "Woe (condemnation) unto them that are wise
    in their _____ eyes, and prudent in their _____ sight!" Proverbs
    14:12 also declares, "There is a way which _____ right unto a
    man, but the end thereof are the ways of _____." There are those
    who are convinced that God doesn't exist, and they pretend to know
    more than what God teaches in His Word, the Bible.

3. Many deny the fact that someday they will have to give an account to
    God. In Hebrews 4:12–13 God affirms, "For the word of God is quick,
    and powerful, and sharper than any twoedged sword, piercing even to
    the dividing asunder of soul and spirit, and of the joints and marrow,
    and is a discerner of the _____ and _____ of the heart. Nei-
    ther is there any creature that is not manifest in his sight: but all things
    are _____ and _____ unto the eyes of him with whom we have to
    do." 1 Timothy 5: 24 declares: "Some men's _____ are open before-
    hand, going before to judgment; and some men they follow after." Also
    Number 32:23 says: "be sure your _____ will find you out." Can we
    possibly deceive God? _____

4. There are those who desire to hide their activities from God, thinking
    that He doesn't pay attention to details. Read Luke 12:1–5.

    a. What does God think of the way you live? _____
        _____ Is there something in your life that you would
        like to hide from God? _____ If it were possible, what would it be?
        _____ How would you do it? _____ Since it is impos-
        sible, should we try to forget or ignore the problem of sin in our life?

22

_____ Why? _____

_____

b. What do you have to do to change what God sees in your life? _____

_____

c. Most of the time we feel more worried about what others think about us and little as to what God sees in us. Why? _____

_____

VIII. How do you see your own condition?

• Read Romans 6:16 and John 8:34.

1. Do you understand what your condition is before God? ____ What is it? _____

2. Do you want to continue on the same course, or do you want to change?

_____

In light of what we have read in God' Word, what type of a sinner do you consider yourself? *Put an "X" on the line as you see yourself.*

1. Little ____   2. Better than most ____   3. Average ____
4. A lot ____   or   5. A terrible sinner ____.

What kind of a sinner are you in the sight of God? _____

_____

Summary:

1. Why did Jesus Christ come to this world? The Apostle Paul gives the reason in 1 Timothy 1:15: "Jesus Christ came into the world to _____ sinners; of whom I am _____."

2. For whom did Jesus Christ die? Romans 5:6 states, "For when we were yet without strength (powerless), in due time Christ died for the _____."

3. Romans 5:8 confirms: "But God commendeth his love toward us, in that, while we were yet sinners, Christ died for _____."

4. Jesus Christ said in John 3:16: "For God so _____ the world (you and me), that he gave his only begotten Son, that whosoever _____

23

(fully trust) in him should not perish, but have everlasting life." Why did Jesus Christ die for us? _____

_____

_____

5. Luke 5:32, declares the great truth that Jesus Christ cannot do anything for the person who does not consider himself to be a _____ .

6. Do you consider yourself to be a terrible sinner in God's sight? _____

REVIEW QUESTIONS

Chapter 2 — THE UNIVERSAL PROBLEM: SIN

1. What is the universal problem? _____

2. All human beings in the world are sinners, however, we know that Jesus Christ was not. Is it possible that there was another, who was not a sinner?

_____

3. Why is it necessary for God to judge and punish the sin of everyone?

_____

4. Is it more difficult for people who are very sinful to be saved? _____
Why? _____

_____

5. Is the first step toward salvation, to recognize that I am a terrible sinner?
_____ Why? _____

_____

6. Did Christ come to save bad people, not those who think they are good?
_____ Why? (1 Timothy 1:15) _____

_____

7. In order for God to save us is it sufficient to only recognize that we are terrible sinners, or must we repent of our sin? _____

8. Can Jesus Christ save the sinner who does not truly repent of all his sin?

_____

9. Can God obligate you to repent of your sin against your own will? _____
   Why? _____

   _____

10. If man tries as hard as he can, and behaves the best he can, is he able to gain
    his entrance into heaven by his good works? _____ Why? _____

    _____

11. Is it possible to help God to save us by doing good deeds? _____

12. Is it true that those who have sinned much are farther from salvation than
    those who have sinned little? _____ Why? _____

    _____

Underline the correct answer: (True) or (False)

13. (True) or (False) Good works and good behavior can justify you in God's
    sight.

14. (True) or (False) Religious rituals and good works cannot solve the prob-
    lem of sin. It is only by the redemption that Jesus Christ provided.

15. (True) or (False) We have to pay for our sins doing certain penitence, ac-
    cording to the requirements of the church we attend.

16. (True) or (False) In order to enjoy the salvation that God has provided, first
    we have the great responsibility of recognizing that we are terrible sinners
    and that we cannot save ourselves.

17. (True) or (False) We sin because we are sinners.

18. (True) or (False) We are sinners because we sin.

19. (True) or (False) Legalism, which is strict obedience to laws, cannot pro-
    duce a clean pure life, nor a pure heart.

20. To whom should we confess our sin? (1 John 1:6–9) _____

21. Who can truly forgive our sin? _____

22. Who can cleanse us from all sin? _____

• Please memorize Romans 3:23 and write it in your own words. _____

_____

_____

———————◆▶◀◆———————

Note: Do you have a person to help you study these lessons? If not, please send your answers to the review questions, along with any doubts, to the Bible Institute Correspondence Department: philippi@becoming-a-christian.org If you prefer, you may to send your letter by U.S. Postal Service to:

Pastor Myron L. Philippi
P.O. Box 1246
Decatur, AL 35602

Do you really know the condition of your own heart? Study carefully the following chapter.

— Chapter Three —

Examining the Heart

The heart is deceitful above all things, and desperately wicked:
who can know it? I the LORD search the heart, I try the reins,
even to give every man according to his ways,
and according to the fruit of his doings. Jeremiah 7:9–10

What does the Bible say about the heart?

The Bible speaks much about the heart of man and also the heart of God. What do we learn in 1 Samuel 16:7? "The LORD _____ not as man _____; for man _____ on the outward appearance, but the LORD _____ on the heart." How do we form opinions about a person?_____ _____ How does God see that same person? _____ _____

Read Mark 7:20–23 to comprehend the condition of the human heart. Christ said: "That which cometh out of the man, that defileth the man. For from _____, out of the heart of men, proceed evil thoughts, adulteries, fornications, murders, thefts, covetousness, wickedness, deceit, lasciviousness, an evil eye, blasphemy, pride, foolishness: All these _____ things come from _____, and _____ the man."

I. The definition of the heart

Proverbs 4:20–23 gives the admonition, "My son, attend to my words; incline thine ear unto my sayings. Let them not depart from thine eyes; keep them in the midst of thine _____. For they are life unto those that find them, and health to all their flesh. Keep thy ____ _____ with all diligence; for out of it are the issues of life." Proverbs 28:25–26 declares,

27

"He that is of a proud _____ stirreth up strife...He that trusteth in his own _____ is a fool."

Underline the statement which best describes the Biblical use of the word "heart."

1. It is the organ that pumps the blood in the body.

2. It is the interior life of man, the soul (his person).

3. It is the visible behavior of the person.

II. The condition of the heart without Christ Jesus

• Read Jeremiah 17:9–10.

1. What were the words that Jeremiah used to describe the heart?_____

   _____

2. Who examines the condition of our heart? _____

3. Why does God need to examine our heart? _____

   _____

III. The contamination of the heart

We read in Matthew 15:1–10, about the religious leaders using the traditions of their religion to make exemptions to the Laws of God. This passage has to do with the obligation that the children have to help the parents and to support the aged. By carrying out a religious ceremony, the priests made the children exempt.

Many religious people give value to the exterior, the practices, and religious traditions, but little importance to the Word of God and the condition of the heart. On one occasion the religious leaders accused Christ and His disciples for not performing the ceremonial washing of the hands before they ate. Read Matthew 15:11–20.

1. Is it possible to contaminate our soul before God if we eat food that is not clean? _____

2. Is it possible to contaminate man's soul with what goes out of the mouth?_____ Why?_____

   _____

3. Where do the sins that we commit originate? _____

   _____

4. According to Matthew 15:19, name one sin that is internal. _____

_____

5. State six sins that are mentioned in verse 19 that are external (visible), which originate in the heart.

   a. _____

   b. _____

   c. _____

   d. _____

   e. _____

   f. _____

6. Where do we find the root of our wickedness? Is it found in the interior (what we are), or in the exterior (what we do)? _____ _____

IV. The cure for the wicked heart

• Read Psalm 51:10, and underline the correct answers.

1. We have to deal with the origin of our actions which is: (the heart), (the mind), (our parents) or (the Bible).

2. We need to let our actions and attitudes be exposed to the Light by: (the preaching of the Word of God), (the Holy Spirit), (reading the Bible) or (all of the above).

3. We need to do more than recognize that there is wickedness in our heart. We need to pay attention to what (society), (education), (religion), or (the Word of God) says to find the solution.

4. According to Matthew 5:8, what is the prerequisite to see God? _____

_____

5. Read Matthew 23:25–28 about the cleansing of the cup (our life), which illustrates the necessity of a total cleansing.

   a. What is the significance of the statement, *which is within the cup and platter?* _____

   b. What is the significance of the statement, *outside of the cup and of the platter?* _____

29

V. The relationship between the heart and its fruits

In Matthew 7:16–20, Christ uses the illustration of the tree and its fruit to show the relationship between our behavior, and our heart, our true life. The tree has roots, trunk, branches, leaves and fruit. There are parts seen and parts not seen.

1. What part of the tree represents the conduct of man? _____

2. What part of the tree represents the heart? _____

3. What kind of fruit does a bad tree produce? _____

4. What kind of fruit does a good tree produce? _____

5. What is the result of having a wicked heart? _____
   _____

6. If you remove the bad fruit from a tree, and put good fruit on it, will it become a good tree? _____

7. Is it possible to grow oranges on apple trees? _____ Is it possible to produce fruit in our life which is contrary to our nature? _____

8. If a person reforms his bad conduct by replacing it with good conduct, will the results be a good person in the sight of God? _____

9. If a person receives a new heart from God, what "fruit" will result in his life? _____

VI. The cleansing of the heart in vain

Many try to clean up their lives by means of religion, rites, good works, and good conduct. Matthew 12:43–45 gives the example of a clean, but empty house.

1. After the wicked spirit had left the body and life of the individual, what was the condition of his heart? _____

2. Did he have a permanent victory over a wicked spirit and sin? _____

3. When a person gets the victory over a certain sin in his life, without giving his life to Christ and becoming His property, what can happen?
   _____

4. What two words spoken by the evil spirit in verse 44 show that the person was not of Christ Jesus? "I will return into ____ _____ " The

temporal change found was only done by the individual's own strength, or the mere fact that the evil spirit wanted to leave in order to carry out a plan and create a situation worse than before.

5. Why did the house stay temporarily garnished (adorned) and clean?
   _____

   What do the garnished things represent? _____
   _____

6. Does a reformation in the individual's life result in a complete transformation or something that is only temporal? _____
   Why?_____

REVIEW QUESTIONS

Chapter 3 — EXAMINING THE HEART

Answer Yes or No.

1. Does sin have its origin in the heart? _____

2. Is it possible to worship God with your mouth and at the same time have your heart far from God? _____

3. Does God have more interest in what we do, or what we appear to be to men, than what is in our heart? _____

4. Is it possible that God is aware of the condition of your heart? _____

5. If your heart and life have been cleansed by God, will your life reflect that cleansing? _____

6. Many religious practices are external. Can they ever correct the evil that is in our hearts? _____

7. Can a person, by his own efforts, have victory over bad habits in order to cleanse his heart? _____

8. Will that which comes from the mouth show what is in the heart? _____

9. Is it possible to change our bad actions by our own strength, and therefore result in a better behavior? _____

10. Will a good behavior be permanent if it comes through reform? _____

11. Can God create in us a new heart so that we can have a new life, which will change our bad behavior? _____ Is this new life permanent? _____

• Please memorize Jeremiah 17:9–10 and write it in your own words. _____

_____

_____

_____

• Ezekiel 11:19–20 declares: "And I will give them one _____, and I will put a new spirit within you; and I will take the stony _____ out of their flesh, and will give them an _____ of flesh: That they may walk in my statutes, and keep mine ordinances, and do them: and they shall be my people, and I will be their God."

• In what way can you have a new *heart* that is truly changed by God? Please explain briefly what you understand on this subject._____

_____

_____

_____

If you do not attend a church that is faithfully teaching the Word of God, we would like to recommend a church in your area where you can hear the teaching of the sound doctrine of the Word of God. Please contact me at the following address: philippi@becoming-a-christian.org

Note: If you do not have a person to help you study these lessons, please send your answers to the review questions and any doubts that you might have regarding this lesson to the Bible Institute Correspondence Department: philippi@becoming-a-christian.org

— Chapter Four —

Who are the Sons of God?

He came unto His own, and his own received Him not.
But as many as received Him, to them gave he power to become
the sons of God, even to them that believe on His name. John 1:11–12

Note: The word "received" is the result of depositing your confidence completely in Him.

Is everyone a son of God?

Everyone has his own opinion as to the form to reach out to God. Many insist that all human beings are sons of God because they have been born into a religious family, have been baptized, or just because they are sons of Adam. Even though all of these "sources of authority" occupy a predominate place in their lives, the true source of authority for man is only the written Word of God, the Holy Bible. Not everyone is a child of God! John 1:12 states clearly that we must become the sons of God.

I. The authority of God's Word is against human philosophies.

1. What man affirms

There are many who believe that all religions will take you to the same God. It simply isn't the truth. Those who make such a declaration have little concept of all religions. Some beliefs do not admit the existence of a Superior Being! However, many feel that every human being is a "child" of God, or that God will have compassion on them in the final judgment. They believe that God is so loving that He would not send them to eternal condemnation, for they do not consider themselves to be all that bad.

There are three principle sources that the majority maintain as their religious authority. As a basis for knowing God, they rely on their *intelligence, their experiences, or their traditions*. This is all that man can rely on when he does not have the truth of God's Word.

a. Their faith is based upon **their intellect**.

It is possible that a family member or a friend has planted doubts in your mind about God and His Word. They seek to promote great intellectual experiences such as existentialism, metaphysics, or cybernetics, which are all philosophies of men. They are nourishing their own egos. Some very sincere people say they are guided by the conscience. One should not forget that he might be very sincere, and at the same time be sincerely mistaken. The conscience is not a reliable guide, unless it is totally governed by the truth of the Word of God. The conscience is directed by what we believe. The only true guide is the light of the Word of God, the Bible. The Psalmist declared in Psalm 119:105, "Thy word is a lamp unto my feet, and a _____ unto my path."

b. Their faith is based upon **their experiences**.

There are those who look for sensational experiences, such as special visions and revelations. They affirm that these unusual experiences "are from God." Their confidence is in themselves and their experiences, not in God. They are also nourishing their own egos with deception.

The Apostles Peter, James, and John had an unforgettable experience when they saw Jesus Christ transfigured before their eyes on the Mount of Transfiguration. In 2 Peter 1:16–21, the Apostle Peter declared: "For we have not followed cunningly _____ fables, when we made known unto you the power and coming of our Lord Jesus Christ, but were _____ of his majesty. For he received from God the Father honor and glory, when there came such a _____ to him from the excellent glory, This is my beloved Son, in whom I am well pleased. And this voice which came from heaven we _____, when we were with him in the holy mount. We have also a more _____ word of prophecy; whereunto ye do well that ye take heed, as unto a light that shineth in a dark place, until the day dawn, and the day star arise in your hearts: Knowing this first, that _____ prophecy of the Scripture is of any private (personal) interpretation. For the prophecy came not in old time by the will of man: but holy men of God spake as they were _____ (inspired) by the Holy Ghost."

c. Their faith is based upon the **traditions of their religion.**
Many put their faith in the traditions of the church and try to stand firm on what their religion teaches. It is an act of depositing a **blind faith** in their religion, in their beliefs, in the sacraments, and rites, trying to gain their salvation. They are taught that it is a sin to doubt any teaching of their religion.

The Lord Jesus Christ taught in Mark 7:7–9: "Howbeit in vain do they worship me, _____ for doctrines the commandments of men. For laying aside the commandment of God, ye hold the _____ of men, as the washing of pots and cups: and many other such like things ye do. And he said unto them, Full well ye reject the commandment of God, that ye may keep your own _____."

2. The only source of <u>authority</u> is the Word of God.
In Matthew 7:13–14, Jesus Christ taught them the only way that truly leads us to God: "Enter ye in at the strait gate: for _____ is the gate, and broad is the way, that leadeth to destruction, and _____ there be which go in thereat: Because _____ is the gate, and _____ is the way, which leadeth unto life, and _____ there be that find it." In order that there be no confusion as to the only way to God, Jesus Christ declared in John 14:6, "I am the _____, the truth, and the life: no man cometh unto the Father, but by _____."

In view of the fact that Satan is the deceiver, he has introduced his teachings, claiming that the *broad way* also leads to heaven. The devil always twists and distorts the Word of God. Peter declared in 2 Peter 3:16, that some of the Scripture written by the Apostle Paul, is "hard to be understood, which they that are unlearned and unstable _____ (twist), as they do also the other _____, unto their own destruction."

The majority of religions teach that there is life after death (the existence of the soul and spirit), but only the Bible teaches that there is eternal life for the true believers in Christ Jesus as their Savior. It is a real and tangible life with body, soul, and spirit. The Apostle Paul warns us in Colossians 2:8, "Beware lest any man spoil you through _____ and vain _____, after the _____ of men, after the rudiments of the world, and not after _____." Many sincere people have a system of beliefs, but do not know or understand what it is to have a close fellowship with Jesus Christ, or what eternal life with Him is all about. Carefully examine your heart with the following questions.

a. Is your faith based on your intelligence?____ The mind of man **cannot be the ultimate judge of the truth.**

b. Is your faith based on experiences? _____ The activities and experiences of man **cannot** be the concluding source of the truth.

c. Is your faith based on religious traditions? _____ Man's religious rites and traditions **cannot draw us nearer to God. There is nothing more reliable than the authority of God's Word.**

II. God gave His plan, but man distorted it.

• Please read John 8:39–47.

1. What opinion did these people have about their relationship with God?

_____

2. Was God their father? _____

3. Who was their father? _____

4. Are all those who believe that they are sons of God really the sons of God? _____

5. Because one believes that God is his Father, does that make it so? _____ Why? _____

6. How can we know that God is really our Father? _____

_____

7. There are only two families (two fathers) in the world. Who are they? (Romans 9:8; John 8:42–44)

a. Family of _____

b. Family of _____

8. There are those who do not want to hear the Word of God. Why?

_____

• Read Genesis 2:7, 21–22

9. Is God the creator of Adam and Eve? _____

10. When Adam and Eve sinned, did they receive a sin nature? _____

11. Because we are descendants of Adam and Eve, does this mean they are our ancestors, and we have received from them their sinful nature? _____

12. What is the difference between being parents and creator?

a. The parents are _____.

b. The creator is _____.

13. Since God only created Adam and Eve, is it God's fault that the human race continues to be born in sin? _____ Why? _____

_____

III. God explains His plan of salvation.

• Read John 3:1–10.

1. What do we know about Nicodemus?

a. He was a _____.

b. He was a _____.

c. He came to Jesus at _____.

2. Being a religious leader, what concept did he have in order to enter heaven? _____

3. What indispensable prerequisite did Jesus give Nicodemus to be able to enter into the kingdom of heaven? _____

4. What were the two questions with sarcasm that Nicodemus directed to Jesus? _____

_____

_____

5. To help Nicodemus understand more clearly, Jesus Christ spoke of two different types of births. We see this in John 3:6. What are they? _____ and _____ We should not confuse or mix the two types of births. The one was totally physical, and the other was totally the work of God.

6. The spiritual birth of which Jesus spoke had two factors, and without them it was impossible to be saved. It says in John 3:5, "Except a man be born of _____ and of the _____, he cannot enter into the kingdom of God."

7. In many parts of the Bible, "water" refers to the Word of God. It does not refer to physical water. What type of "water" is it talking about here? _____

8. In John 4:7–14, Jesus carefully explains that He was not talking about physical water. To what class of water was he referring? _____

9. Ephesians 5:26, declares that the Christian is sanctified and cleansed "with the washing of water by the _____."

10. James 1:18 and 1 Peter 1:23 talk about a new birth by the _____ _____.

11. By means of these passages we see that the "water" is the _____ _____.

12. In John 3:3 and 7, Jesus Christ lets us clearly see that it is indispensable for us to be born _____ so that we can enter into the Kingdom of God.

13. This new birth takes place by means of "water," which is the _____ of God and by the work of the Holy _____ of God.

14. The people who have only the first birth are of the family of _____.

15. The people who have had the second birth are of the family of _____.

16. Is it possible to enter into the Kingdom of God by only having experienced the first birth? _____ Why? _____

_____

17. What is the difference between the new birth and a reform? The new birth is _____. The reform is: _____.

18. In our first birth (physical), of whom are we sons? _____

19. In our second birth (spiritual), of whom are we sons? _____

20. Is it possible for a person to reform his old nature by his good works sufficiently in order to enter into God's heaven? _____ How? _____

_____

IV. God's plan is easy to understand.

1. John 1:12 clearly states the need "to _____ the sons of God." It is not something that we can do by our own will or capacity, but it is by the work of God through His Word. Here it teaches that the action of "receive" is the result of having deposited our total confidence in Jesus Christ as our personal Savior. He **receives** us as a member of His family.

2. John 1:13 declares that it is impossible to become a son of God by being born of **"blood."** In other words, being born into a Christian family does not make you a Christian, any more than one's father being a carpenter, would make him a carpenter. Salvation does not come through heritage from a good family. True salvation does not take place through physical _____, but through a spiritual _____.

3. John 1:13 also teaches that the **"new birth"** is not something that someone else can do for you. God has to do it. Jesus Christ affirms that it is not **"of the will of the _____."** It is not a result of our works, personal reform, religious rites, or traditions.

4. The Apostle John continues by saying **"nor of the will of man."** In other words, we can do nothing to save someone else. We can teach them, warn them, and give them the Gospel message, but we cannot <u>make</u> someone believe! True faith only comes through God's Word and God has to bring conviction of sin and a real repentance for that sin. There is no way to change the destiny of man after he dies.

5. The only solution for the lost condition of mankind is completely remote from our human capabilities. In John 1:13 the Word of God discloses that it is only by the **"grace of _____"** that we can be saved. God has to do the work of saving us. There is **NOTHING** that we can do of ourselves to be saved.

V. God provided salvation for all.

1. Through a miracle, God, the Second Person of the Deity, received a human body, and the virgin Mary gave birth to Jesus Christ. John 1:14 declares, "And the Word was made _____, and _____ among us, (and we beheld his glory, the glory as of the only begotten of the Father,) full of grace and truth." Jesus Christ was 100% man and at the same time 100% God.

2. Jesus Christ received upon Himself the sin of the whole world, and gave Himself to die on the cross for our sin. Peter explains in 1 Peter 3:18, "For Christ also hath _____ suffered for sins, the just for the unjust, that he might bring us to God."

3. Jesus Christ physically arose from the dead after being in the tomb three days to assure us of eternal salvation, and to also guarantee that we will some day be resurrected from the dead. Romans 4:25 says, "Who was delivered for our offences, and was _____ again for our justification." The Apostle Paul assured all Christians in 1 Corinthians 15:20, "But now is Christ <u>risen</u> from the dead, and become the first–fruits of them that slept." The Apostle John taught in 1 John 4:2, "Hereby know ye the Spirit of God: Every <u>spirit</u> that confesseth that Jesus Christ is <u>come in the flesh</u> is of God: And every <u>spirit</u> that confesseth not that Jesus Christ is <u>come in the flesh</u> is not of God: and this is that spirit of antichrist, whereof ye have heard that it should come; and even now already is it in the world." Here it mentioned *spirit*, speaking of the *spirit of the teaching or the heart of the teaching*. This passage also mentions *come in the flesh* in reference to the *physical resurrection of Jesus Christ*.

4. Jesus Christ is the only mediator between God the Father and all men. 1 Timothy 2:5–6 affirms: "For there is one God, and one _____ between God and men, the man Christ Jesus; Who gave himself a _____ for all." Jesus is the only substitute for man before God. There is no other!

Summary:

If salvation were possible by fulfilling religious rites, traditions, baptisms, confirmations, religious heritage, personal reforms, or any other physical efforts that mankind might try to do through their own strength, **then Jesus Christ would not have had to die for our sins.** Salvation only comes through the finished work of Jesus Christ. We must be born again to become the sons of God. Also, if salvation could be received by what we could give of our possessions, and our sacrifices, then God would be unjust by not putting the conditions within the reach of all. God is *Faithful and Just* to give the opportunity to all to hear His only true plan of salvation so that we might have fellowship with Him. Only those who repent of their sins, trust Jesus Christ as their personal Savior, and give themselves to Him, are made the sons of God. (John 1:12)

REVIEW QUESTIONS

CHAPTER 4 — WHO ARE THE SONS OF GOD?

Underline the correct answer: (True) or (False)

1. (True) or (False)   God is the Father of all mankind.

2. (True) or (False) The declarations of the Pope, the traditions of the church, and their "holy books" are all superior to the Bible, the Word of God.

3. (True) or (False)   Among all humans, only two classes of people exist, the sons of God and the sons of the devil.

4. (True) or (False)   All human beings are sinners, except for Jesus Christ.

5. (True) or (False) Sin is a universal problem that came from Adam and Eve, which we receive from our parents through physical birth (Romans 5:12).

6. (True) or (False)   Because he loved us, Jesus Christ received upon Himself the sins of the whole world, and then He received the punishment of God the Father for our sins.

7. (True) or (False)   God is the Father of all who believe in Him.

8. (True) or (False)   So that God can be our Father, we have to be born into His family.

9. (True) or (False)   So that God can be our Father, we have to do many good things for others.

10. (True) or (False)   The moment that we become a member of God's family, we receive a new nature.

11. (True) or (False)   When we become sons of God, we receive a new nature that only God, through the Lord Jesus Christ, can give us. (2 Corinthians 5:17)

12. (True) or (False)   The new birth comes only through the Word of God by permitting the Holy Spirit to do His ministry in our heart. He convinces us of the need to repent of our sin and the great need to give ourselves to Christ Jesus with our whole heart.

13. (True) or (False)   There are many people who have been deceived through emotional experiences that temporarily make them feel good about themselves.

14. (True) or (False)   God will accept our emotional experiences as a basis for our salvation.

15. (True) or (False)   After we give ourselves to Jesus Christ, trusting Him as our only sufficient personal Savior, we understand the great necessity to obey Him. (1 Thessalonians 4:1)

16. (True) or (False)   God is the Father only of those who have trusted completely in the Person and work of Jesus Christ, by His death on the cross, where He paid the penalty completely for their sin so that He could become their Savior.

• Please memorize John 1:11–12 and express it in your own words. _____

_____

_____

_____

_____

———————◆◆»◆«◆◆———————

The next lesson helps us to understand what true salvation involves. Please continue.

— Chapter Five —

Salvation: The Spiritual Birth

For by grace are ye saved through faith;
and that not of yourselves: it is the gift of God:
Not of works, lest any man should boast.
Ephesians 2:8–9

In what condition do we find ourselves according to the Word of God?

If a man was shipwrecked in the high sea without a lifesaver, and was at the point of drowning, what would he need? Would he need a few words of encouragement, a better job, more money, a new car, a better house, or a doctor? Of course not! He would need someone that could save him immediately from the danger of drowning. In the same way, the majority of the people in the world are in a lost condition, and heading for an eternity without true salvation. This salvation can only be received through the Lord Jesus Christ. Many are looking for temporal and material things in which to trust. Unfortunately countless are not interested in the Word of God or spiritual things because they do not understand their personal need. In what condition do we find ourselves, according to Ephesians 2:1–3? _____

The "natural" man cannot produce that which is supernatural. It is impossible! Through your own strength, you cannot better your "old nature," nor produce in yourself a "new nature." It is impossible to do anything to please God. This nature only comes from God. Salvation is what God does in and for a person; it is not what man can do for himself. God explains that all need to be saved, and the Word of God tells us how to obtain this salvation.

43

I. We are lost and condemned sinners.

1. Romans 3:10–18 says that all men are lost and on the way to hell, as we saw in the previous lessons. In verses 10 and 11 God says, "There is none _____, no, not one: There is none that _____ _____, there is none that _____ after God." In light of this passage, we see that man is incapable of pleasing God with his life, because he is spiritually dead.

2. The Bible gives us the reason why sinful mankind is under God's judgement and is condemned. John 3:17–20 declares that Christ did not come to condemn anyone to eternal death, because they are already condemned. This passage says: "For God sent not His Son into the world to _____ the world; but that the world through him might be saved. He that believeth (deposit all his confidence in) on him is not condemned: but he that believeth not is _____ already, because he hath not believed (deposit all his confidence in) in the name of the only begotten Son of God. And this is the condemnation, that light is come into the world, and men loved _____ rather than light, because their deeds were evil."

3. How many people are guilty of being sinners? Romans 3:23 says, "For _____ have sinned, and come short of the glory of God." This verse teaches that even the best people cannot please God with their lives or with their works, because they are sinners from their conception. It is declared in 1 Peter 1:17, "And if ye call on the Father, who without respect of persons judgeth according to every man's work..." This teaches that God does not make any exceptions. Do you recognize that you are a sinner and need to be saved? _____

4. The Bible tells us that eternal condemnation is only for lost sinners. Romans 6:23 makes clear that the result or "the wages of sin is death." This death is terrible. It is not the destruction or annihilation of the soul. To what kind of death does this refer? _____

What does "death" signify?

a. **Physical death** refers to the separation of the soul and the spirit from the body. When our body remains without life, our soul and spirit will leave our earthly body and continue to live on in its eternal destiny. They never die.

44

b. **Spiritual death** is the state in which man finds himself without Christ. This is the part of man that died when Adam and Eve obeyed Satan, sinned against God and broke their fellowship with Him. Ephesians 2:1 speaks of the death of the spirit of the individual: "And you hath he quickened (made alive), who were _____ in trespasses and sins."

c. **Eternal death** is the destiny of the person that dies physically, without having deposited his confidence with all his heart in Jesus Christ as his Savior. He is separated (soul, spirit, and body) from God forever. This person goes to his eternal destiny without Christ, to the place God calls *Hell*, then later to the *Lake of Fire*. This last class of death is what the Bible calls "eternal condemnation" or "eternal death." Read Revelation 20:14–15.

In contrast, the soul and spirit of the true Christian goes directly with Christ the moment he dies. The Apostle Paul confirmed this in 2 Corinthians 5:8, "absent from the body, and to be present with the _____." Philippians 1:23 affirms that this is *far better*. This is only for those that know Christ Jesus as their personal Savior.

5. In Isaiah 64:6 God declares that all of us are wicked, and terribly lost: "But we are all as an _____ thing, and all our righteousnesses are as _____ rags; and we all do fade as a leaf; and our iniquities, like the wind, have taken us away." How do you see your own spiritual condition? _____ According to the authority of the Bible, how does God see your good works? _____ _____ Do you recognize that you are a lost sinner and in need of salvation? _____

II. We are unable to save ourselves.

1. We are in a spiritual dilemma! Mankind is too weak and is incapable of doing what God requires. If it were possible to be saved by fulfilling the Law of God, we would have to completely obey all of the Law, or it would not be sufficient. James 2:10 confirms this by saying, "For whosoever shall keep the _____ law, and yet offend in one point, he is _____ of all."

2. Ephesians 2:8–9 declares that only God can do the work of saving us: "For by grace are ye saved through faith; and that not of _____:

45

it is the gift of God: not of _____, lest any man should boast." Many people attempt to appear good before men by trying to impress them with their deeds. Others want society to look at them as someone special, to make people think that God looks upon them as a person in favorable standing with Him. They are deceiving themselves, believing that they are gaining favor with God. They try to gain salvation by their works, or by the things that they do, such as attending church, fulfilling certain religious rites, making large contributions, or being a good citizen. They endeavor to be a "good, loving, and respectful person." There is a great desire to give a good impression to the world, thinking that God will be pleased. Can these things save them? _____

3. The "natural man" cannot produce what is supernatural. It is impossible for our old nature with its sinful ways to better itself, produce a new nature, or draw us to God. Salvation is what Jesus Christ does in and for man. What a person can do for himself, does not count with God. God gives us a clear explanation about the glorious salvation that all of us need. He tells us how we can receive it, and be assured that we belong to Christ.

III. God loves us and wants to save us.

1. In spite of our rebellion and sin, God loves us. What was the principal proof of His love? Romans 5:8 says, "But God commendeth His _____ toward us, in that, while we were yet sinners, Christ died for us." Through His teaching of the revelation of Himself throughout the entire Bible, God illustrates His love to all mankind. Do you know that God loves you? _____ How does He show that love to you? _____

_____

2. The will and supreme desire of God is that no one should perish and go to Hell for all eternity. Jesus Christ has done all that is necessary to save the sinner from condemnation. 2 Peter 3:9 says, "The Lord is not slack concerning His promise, as some men count slackness; but is longsuffering to us-ward, not willing that _____ should perish, but that _____ should come to repentance." God does not want you to die without receiving His provision of eternal life. Do you understand that God is patiently waiting for you? _____

3. In spite of our terrible sinful nature God offers us salvation. He wants to save us by His grace. Ephesians 2:8 declares: "For by _____ are ye saved through faith; and that not of yourselves: it is the _____ of God." The definition of the word *grace* is: a gift or consideration that we do not deserve from God. Salvation is a gift from God that we do not deserve, because of what we are, or what we have done. Romans 5:20–21 explains that "where sin abounded, _____ did much more abound. That as sin hath reigned unto death, even so might _____ reign through righteousness unto eternal life by Jesus Christ our Lord." Even though it is a gift of God for us, it cost the Lord Jesus Christ the great price of suffering death on the cross for our sins. He received the terrible just judgment of God in our place. In reality, we are worthy of eternal condemnation in the Lake of Fire, as mentioned in Revelations 20:15. Do you understand that even though you do not deserve anything good, God wants to show you His grace?_____

4. If it were not for the mercy of God, all of us would go to hell, because it is what we deserve for our wicked deeds. We all deserve eternal condemnation in the Lake of Fire (Revelation 20:15). Ephesians 2:4–5 declares, "But God, who is rich in _____, for His great _____ wherewith he loved us, even when we were dead in sins, hath quickened us together with Christ, (by grace ye are saved)." James 5:11 also affirms: "The Lord is very pitiful, and of tender _____." The word, *mercy,* means that God does not give to us what we deserve. Psalm 103:8 shows us the character of God: "The LORD is merciful and gracious, slow to anger, and plenteous in _____." Do you understand that even though you merit eternal damnation, God wants to show you, in a very special way, His mercy? _____

IV. The provision of God is Jesus Christ.

1. God gave us His only Son, showing His great love for us. John 3:16 says, "For God so _____ the _____ (you and me), that he gave His only begotten Son, that whosoever _____ in him should not perish, but have everlasting life." The word *believe* means — it is the act of putting your complete confidence in Christ Jesus for salvation.

2. Christ Jesus took our place and died for us, taking all of our sin on Himself. The prophecy in Isaiah 53:6 declares what Jesus Christ did for us:

47

"All we like _____ have gone astray; we have turned every one to his ____ way; and the LORD hath laid on Him the iniquity of us all." God the Father poured out His wrath upon Jesus Christ, who shed His blood on the cross, was punished in our place in payment for sin. Even though salvation is a gift of God, the supreme price had to be paid. Jesus Christ received our sins upon Himself, suffered, and died on the cross for our redemption. His terrible death shows the awfulness of our sin.

3. Jesus Christ died, was buried in a tomb and after three days physically arose from the dead to assure us that He has the power to save us and cleanse us from all wickedness. In brief, this is the glorious and victorious message of the Gospel of the Lord Jesus Christ. Paul proclaimed this message in 1 Corinthians 15:3–4: "For I delivered unto you first of all that which I also received, how that Christ _____ for our sins according to the Scriptures; and that he was _____, and that he _____ again the third day according to the Scriptures." It is indispensable to believe in the physical resurrection of Jesus Christ; otherwise it would be impossible to have the assurance of our salvation. Are you convinced of the physical resurrection of our Lord Jesus Christ? _____

4. After forty days, Jesus Christ physically ascended to heaven, sat at the right hand of God the Father, and is now mediator between God and man. (1 Timothy 2:5) There is no other who can mediate for us before God. Verse 6 explains the reason why Jesus Christ is the only mediator. "Who gave _____ a ransom for all, to be testified in due time." We should not be confused between the word, *intercessor* and *mediator*. In this case a *mediator* indicates that only He could obtain for us salvation by His complete work on the cross to give us His pardon. The Holy Spirit intercedes for us and we should intercede for others.

V. It is easy to understand God's plan of salvation.

Ephesians 2:8–9, teaches us two things that cannot save us. What are they?
1. _____ 2. _____

God's provision of salvation does not come to us because of what we do or what we are. We are not saved by our own faith. If it is not our faith, then how are we saved? Galatians 2:16 declares that the justification that God gives does not come through anything that we can do in the way of good works, and it is not through our own faith that we are saved, but through the faith of Jesus Christ: "Knowing that a man is not _____ by the _____ of the law, but by the _____ of <u>Jesus</u> <u>Christ</u>, even we have believed in Jesus Christ, that we might be justified by the _____ of <u>Christ</u>, and not by the works of the law: for by the works of the law shall no flesh be justified." So many feel that they have a great faith created and promoted by their own will, or through their religion; however, God declares that it is impossible for that kind of faith to save us. According to God's Word, **it is only through the faith that the Lord Jesus Christ imparts to us that we can truly deposit our full confidence in Him**. What does God's Word command us to do?

1. <u>Receive the "faith of God."</u>

   It is first necessary to hear the Word of God to be able to believe God. Romans 10:17 insists that this faith is not our faith, but the faith that comes through the Word of God: "So then _____ cometh by _____, and hearing by the _____ of God." In Romans 4:3 the Apostle Paul spoke of the salvation of Abraham of the Old Testament, and how he received his righteousness; "Abraham believed God, and it was counted unto him for _____." If we believe God, we deposit our confidence in who God is, what He says in His Word, and in what He did for us. Therefore, we must deposit our complete faith and confidence in Jesus Christ, God the Son, for what He has done through his death and resurrection from the dead to pardon us from our sins and give us eternal life. This signifies that this faith can only come from Christ through the Word of God, the Bible. For whom did Jesus do this? He did it for _____.

2. <u>Believe the Word of God.</u>

   The word *believe* imports much more meaning than just a simple recognition of facts or truths. The problem of many is that they only want to believe "something" that is nothing more than a creed. In the Greek, the language in which the New Testament was written, we see that the word *believe* is the act of "**depositing your faith completely.**" In this case we must deposit our complete confidence in what God says in His Word. 1 John 5:10 says, "He that _____ on the Son of God hath the witness in himself: he that believeth not God, (the person that believes not) hath made him a _____; because he believeth not the

_____ that God gave of His Son." Those who do not believe God are declaring that God is a liar. Give careful attention to what Jesus said in John 3:17–21. Do you believe what the Word of God says?

_____

3. Recognize that you are a wicked sinner.
Because of the sinners that we are, we have to recognize and admit our lost condition. We were born sinners, and therefore have a sinful nature. God sees us as we are: vile and terrible sinners. We sin because we are terrible lost sinners. If there exists any doubt regarding this, study once again Chapters 2 and 3. Read carefully Romans 3:10–18, 23, and James 2:10. How does God see us?_____

4. Repent of all your sins.
Jesus Christ said that we have to sincerely repent of our sins with all of our heart (Mark 1:15; Luke 3:8; Luke 24:47). The servants of God wrote and preached about the need for true repentance. True repentance is not part of faith, but it comes in the same way as faith, through the Word of God. The word *baptism* is used in Mark 1:4 to teach that there has to be a complete submersion in repentance on our part. (Read other corresponding passages: 2 Peter 3:9; Romans 2:4; Mark 6:12; Acts 3:19; 5:31; 11:18; 20:21)

What is repentance? It is all of the following:

- Read Jeremiah 8:6.
  Repentance is a change of thought (mind and attitude) about our way of being, acting and living.

- Read Job 42:6.
  Repentance is a change of heart toward sin for the purpose of recognizing and judging sin for what it is: wicked and terrible.

- Read Mark 12:30.
  Repentance is a change of heart toward God to love Him.

- Read 2 Corinthians 7:9–10.
  Repentance is a genuine sorrow for the sin that we have committed against God.

  a. We have to understand that the death of Jesus Christ paid our full debt with God, but just because it is paid, does not mean that we have received that pardon or forgiveness. The Lord Jesus gives the command in Luke 13:24, "_____ to enter in at the strait gate." The word *strive* in Greek is "agonize," which denotes nothing less than true repentance.

b. What happens if you do not truly repent? The only alternative is the condemnation of eternal death in the Lake of Fire. Read carefully once again, 2 Corinthians 7:10. "For godly sorrow worketh repentance to salvation not to be repented of: but the sorrow of the world worketh _____." The death that is referred to here is eternal death. They will receive the punishment of God for sin in *Hell*, and afterwards they will be judged at the Great White Throne where they will proceed to the *Lake of Fire* for all eternity. (Revelation 20:11–15) The explanation is given in Romans 2:5–6, "But after thy hardness and _____ heart treasurest up unto thyself wrath against the day of wrath and revelation of the righteous judgment of God; Who will render to every man according to his _____."

c. Do you love your sin and this worldly system in which we live? Carefully read 1 John 1:9, and notice that Jesus Christ "is _____ and _____ to forgive us our sins, and to cleanse us from all unrighteousness." **God wants to cleanse us from all sin and evil**, but if someone is rebellious and does not want to be cleansed, or does not want to leave their sins, **God cannot save him.** The love and adoration for those sins (bad habits) is actually idolatry, which is an abomination to God. If you **love your sin**, you do not love God. God categorically declares that there is no fellowship between God and the things of the worldly system. He demands in 2 Corinthians 6:14–16, "Be ye not unequally _____ together with unbelievers: for what fellowship hath righteousness with unrighteousness? And what communion hath _____ with _____? And what concord hath Christ with Belial? Or what part hath he that believeth with an infidel? And what agreement hath the temple of God with idols?" Again, 1 John 2:15 gives emphasis saying: "Love not the _____, neither the things that are in the world. If any man _____ the world, **the love of the Father is not in him.**" God gave us the eternal commandment in Exodus

20:2–5 saying, "I am the Lord thy God, which have brought thee out of the land of Egypt, out of the house of bondage. Thou shalt have no other gods before me. Thou shalt not make unto thee any graven _____, or any likeness of any thing that is in heaven above, or that is in the earth beneath, or that is in the water under the earth. Thou shalt not _____ down thyself to them, nor _____ them: for I the Lord thy God am a jealous God, visiting the iniquity of the fathers upon the children unto the third and fourth generation of them that hate me." This terrible chain of condemnation ends when that "one" obeys God.

d. Is it possible to believe the works and data concerning the Lord Jesus Christ and at the same time not be saved? _____ The Apostle Paul warned the Corinthian church of this problem in 2 Corinthians 13:5 saying, "_____yourselves, whether ye be in the faith; _____ your own selves. Know ye not your own selves, how that Jesus Christ is in you, except ye be reprobates?" The reason was obvious. There were many members in the church who were not saved. 2 Corinthians 6:1 tells us to "receive not the grace of God in _____." There are those that give mental consent, saying that they believe in God, but they are in a lost condition, because they have not repented of their sin and have not given themselves to Jesus Christ with all their heart. Many have a <u>false security</u> because they have made a <u>superficial</u> <u>decision</u> to *accept or receive Christ*. This results in *easy–believism*, and is only a mere profession with the mouth and not with the heart.

e. Can the Word of God bring repentance to us? **Yes!** It is the only repentance that God recognizes for our salvation. Paul declared in 2 Corinthians 7:9, "Now I rejoice, not that ye were made sorry, but that ye sorrowed to _____: for ye were made sorry after a _____ manner." This passage teaches that repentance comes from the Word of God. True repentance comes in the same manner as the true "faith of God." Romans 10:17 declares: "So then _____ cometh by hearing, and hearing by the word of God." Can we have true repentance only by being very sorry for our sin?

_____

52

5. <u>Believe with all your heart</u>

It is imperative to believe with all our heart (in the deepest part of our being) that Christ Jesus died on the cross to take the punishment of God for our sins, and after three days physically arose in order to save us. In the letter of Apostle Paul in Romans 10:9–10 he declares, "That if thou shalt confess with thy mouth the Lord Jesus, and shalt believe in thine heart that God hath _____ him from the dead, thou shalt be saved. For with the _____ man believeth unto righteousness; and with the mouth confession is made unto _____." The punishment that we deserve, Christ took upon Himself. He is our substitute. He took our place to free us from eternal punishment and to give us forgiveness of sin.

6. <u>Ask God to forgive your sins.</u>

We have to ask God with all sincerity in prayer to forgive us for our sins through Christ who is the only sufficient Savior. In Luke 18:13, the publican, who prayed in the temple, felt a profound repentance for his sin, and expressed: "And the publican, standing afar off, would not lift up so much as his _____ unto heaven, but smote upon his breast, saying, God be _____ to me a _____." He asked forgiveness to God with a contrite (repented) heart, and God forgave all his sin. God also wants to forgive all your sin, if you ask him. He wants to forgive us and cleanse us from all sin. 1 John 1:9 states: "If we confess our sins, He is faithful and _____ to forgive us our _____, and to cleanse us from all unrighteousness."

Do you have a <u>change of thinking</u> and attitude regarding yourself and your life? Do you recognize your sin, and have a <u>change of heart</u> for what it is, bad and terrible? Do you have a true <u>change of heart</u> toward God to love Him, and a genuine sadness for sin that you have committed against God? _____ God wants to cleanse you from all sin. 1 John 1:9–10 reminds us, that "If we _____ our sins (to Christ), he is _____ and _____ to forgive us our sins, and to cleanse us from all unrighteousness. If we say that we have not sinned, we make him a _____, and his _____ is not in us." If you do not want to be cleansed, or if you love your sin and do not want to abandon your sin, can God do a work in your life against your will? _____ Can God save you when your love is directed toward what God hates? _____

Do you love what God hates and hate what God loves? _____ If you love the sin that God hates, will God ignore what you are doing?

_____

7. Give yourself with all your heart to Jesus Christ.

Besides many other passages in the Bible, we read in 1 Corinthians 6:19–20 that we have to become the property of God forever. Paul asked the question, "What? know ye not that your body is the temple of the Holy Ghost which is in you, which ye have of God, and ye are _____ your own? For ye are _____ with a price: therefore glorify God in your body, and in your spirit, which are _____." We no longer belong to ourselves, and much less to Satan and this world's system. Those who want to be saved have to give themselves completely to Christ in order to become His property. If you belong to Jesus Christ, then you will desire to live according to His desires and the Word of God.

Romans 6:17–18 explains what happens when a person gives himself to Christ Jesus with all of his heart. The Apostle Paul announced, "But God be thanked, that ye were the _____ of sin, but ye have _____ from the heart that form of doctrine (*doctrine* refers to Jesus Christ) which was _____ you." The original text states "to whom we are delivered." There is only one of two who you can have as owner of your life, Jesus Christ or Satan. Of whom are you a slave?

_____

Jesus Christ is the central figure of all Bible doctrine, and because of this it has to be your own decision to give yourselves to Christ Jesus, so that He will be the center of your life. God demands direct obedience to Christ with all our heart.

VI. Is it possible to believe in secret?

Is it possible that someone upon repenting of all his sins, giving himself to Christ with all his heart, loving Him with all his being, can at the same time be a Christian in secret? _____ Matthew 10:32–33 says, "Whosoever therefore shall confess me _____ men, him will I confess also _____ my Father which is in heaven. But whosoever shall deny me before men, him will I also deny before my Father which is in heaven." Here the word *confess* means – *the act of giving testimony that we belong to Him*. It is difficult to understand why someone would not be willing to renounce his old life, and begin a new life with Jesus Christ. We realize there are pressures that come from the family, religious organizations, the society, the work place, and at times the government, but never can a cowardly attitude be justified on the part of a true believer. When we trust the Lord Jesus Christ as our personal Savior, we can never deny Him to the world around us. Upon reading John 12:42–43, we understand that God requires firmness as we consider the words of Jesus: "Nevertheless among the chief rulers also many believed on him; but because of the Pharisees they did not _____ him, lest they should be put _____ of the synagogue: for they loved the praise of _____ more than the praise of God." In Romans 1:16, Paul declared, "For I am not _____ of the gospel of Christ: for it is the power of God unto salvation to every one that believeth; to the Jew first, and also to the Greek." Is it possible to be a secret believer? _____ (Romans 9:33; 10:9–11)

Summary:

True faith in Jesus Christ as our only sufficient Lord and Savior comes from God and through the Word of God. The Holy Spirit of God guides us to believe and trust in Jesus Christ and moves us to react correctly. **This action of faith in Christ Jesus brings true repentance, and our giving of ourselves completely to Him. He has to be pre-eminent and not just prominent in our life. Can this happen only by attending Bible studies? No! Can someone else make this decision for you? No!** This is your decision, not to be made by another. Your children cannot do it for you. Your parents cannot do it for you. Your relatives cannot do it for you. You must make the decision yourself. It is important to read God's Word, attend Bible studies and hear God's Word faithfully preached in church services so that God can do His work is your heart. Do you remember how true faith comes to us, as declared by the Apostle Paul in Romans 10:17? "So then faith cometh by _____, and hearing by the _____ of God." The Bible is the instrument that God uses to enable you to understand His true plan for salvation, and then "grow in grace, and in the knowledge of our Lord and Savior Jesus Christ." (2 Peter 3:18)

STOP!

VII. It costs a lot to be a disciple of Christ!

Christ Jesus paid the complete price so that we can be saved, but it will cost us dearly if we truly want to follow Him, and be His disciples. Should we enter into a commitment or business transaction without knowing the cost or the consequences of the commitment? _____ Neither should we make a spiritual commitment without considering first what Jesus Christ says in Luke 14 about the future of the true Christian. We never should make a promise to God if we do not mean what we say, or if we do not understand it. Ignorance does not give us an excuse with God. He makes us responsible for our decisions. The commitment to give myself to Christ Jesus requires the understanding of God's plan for salvation. It is not just a decision, a belief, or a prayer because we think that it is something good to do. Since the first century **true Christians** have suffered much persecution because they faithfully followed and obeyed Jesus Christ. Is it possible that we are exempt, just because we live in the 21st century? _____

There are seven basic truths to help us understand the cost of being a true disciple of Jesus Christ. You should understand from the previous studies, that salvation does not come through the following seven items, but it is necessary to know that there is a **cost of discipleship.**

• Read Luke 14:26–33.

1. As a disciple of Christ, <u>we have to hate the worldly system, and above all else, love God</u>.
   Luke 14:26 states, "If any man come to me, and hate not his _____, and _____, and wife, and children, and brethren, and sisters, yea, and his _____ life also, he cannot be my disciple." What does it mean to say, "I need to hate my family?" It does not mean despise them, but rather that we love Jesus Christ more than any other person. The love of a family must appear as if it were hate in comparison to the love that we have for Jesus Christ. Mark 12:30 tells us how we should love God: "And thou shalt love the Lord thy God with _____ thy heart,

56

and with _____ thy soul, and with _____ thy mind, and with all thy strength." How can you love Christ in this way and still love images, traditions, relics or any other thing that we reverenced before? Is it possible to continue in our old life? _____ If we have confidence in these things, the truth is, we do not love God. Read Deuteronomy 7:25. "The graven _____ of their gods shall ye burn with fire: thou shalt not desire the silver or gold that is on them, nor take it unto thee, lest thou be snared therein: for it is an _____ (hatred) to the Lord thy God." What does God hate? _____ _____ What does God require that we do with those things? __ _____

2. As a disciple of Christ, <u>there will be conflicts and divisions in some families because of the Gospel.</u>

   a. Jesus Christ declares in John 3:19, "And this is the condemnation, that _____ is come into the world, and men loved darkness rather than _____, because their deeds were evil." Jesus Christ is the LIGHT. Also Jesus Christ said in John 15:18–20, "If the world hate you, ye know that it hated me _____ it hated you. If ye were of the world, the world would love his own: but because ye are not of the _____, but I have chosen you out of the world, therefore the world hateth you. Remember the word that I said unto you, the servant is not greater than his lord. If they have persecuted me, they will also persecute _____; if they have kept my saying, they will keep yours also."

   b. Our family members, parents, children, uncles, or in-laws are going to think that we are leaving the religion of which they approve. Christ knew that there would be conflicts in the family because of Him. For this reason, He insists that we give ourselves completely to Him. He affirms this in Luke 12:51–53, and Matthew 10:34–38 saying, "And a man's foes shall be they of his _____ household." Jesus Christ does not want it this way. Often the problem is that the family does not know what the Bible says about their own spiritual needs in order to have a personal relationship with Christ Jesus. When there is not true love for Christ in the home, there exists a rejection of those who belong to Christ Jesus. The Christian can and must show even more love and patience for his family than ever before, because the love of Christ now fills his being. We must remember that we can be the instruments that God wants to use so that our family members might be saved. There are no limits to His love (Romans 5:1–5).

3. As a disciple of Christ, <u>we make personal sacrifices</u>. Luke 14:27 speaks of bearing "his _____, and come after me." It is truly a sacrifice of our personal desires for the purpose of following the will of Christ, as shown in the Word of God. When the *cross* is mentioned, it is not speaking of some sickness or difficulty, but a *sacrifice of self* in unconditional obedience to Christ Jesus. In 2 Timothy 3:12 the Apostle Paul declares with certainty: "Yea, and all that will live godly (a life which God requires) in Christ Jesus shall suffer _____." The Apostle Peter reminds us in 1 Peter 1:6–9, that the Christian life is not easy with all its trials and afflictions: "Wherein ye greatly _____, though now for a season, if need be, ye are in heaviness through manifold temptations (testings)." It is a personal sacrifice. Luke 14:27 finishes by saying, "And whosoever doth not bear his cross, and come after me, cannot be my _____."

4. As a disciple of Christ, <u>it is necessary to do an examination of our heart</u>.
It might appear that Luke 14:28–30 is talking about the construction of a tower, but it is not the case. Christ Jesus uses it as an illustration to let us know that it is necessary to count the cost of giving ourselves to Him, of being His disciples and truly following Him. It is a full commitment to Him. If we do not count the cost, **we could turn back,** and become a mockery and an enemy of God. There are those that look at the true Christian and see that his life is peaceful, happy, confident, and pleasant. They want to have what we have, so they make a *decision*, but they are not sincere with God, or with themselves. The Apostle Peter warns us in 2 Peter 2:20–22 of the danger of making a false decision: "For it had been better for them not to have known the way of righteousness, than, after they have known it, to _____ from the holy commandment delivered unto them. But it is happened unto them according to the true proverb, The _____ is turned to his own vomit again; and the _____ that was washed to her wallowing in the mire." Also, our Lord said in Luke 9:62, ". . . No man, having put his hand to the plough, and looking back,

is _____ for the kingdom of God." The act of *having put his hand to the plough*, refers to someone who has made his commitment, repenting of his sins and giving himself wholeheartedly to Jesus Christ. When one is sincere with God and truly born again, nothing or no one can cause him to turn back. The Apostle Paul said in Hebrews 10:39: "But we are not of them who draw_____ unto perdition; but of them that _____ to the saving of the soul."

5. As a disciple of Christ, <u>we will have battles against our enemy, Satan</u>. In Luke 14:31–32, Jesus compares the Christian life with **warfare**. First we must decide whether God can do what He promises. Romans 8:31 says, "What shall we then say to these things? If _____ be for us, who can be _____ us?" The Apostle Paul warns that we must receive help from God in order to be victorious in our battles against Satan. It tells us in Ephesians 6:11–12 to "put on the whole _____ of God, that ye may be able to stand against the _____ of the devil. For we wrestle not against flesh and blood, but against principalities, against powers, against the rulers of the darkness of this world, against spiritual wickedness in high places." If you are under the conviction of the Holy Spirit, but think that the Christian life will be too hard, you should permit God to help you overcome this fear. If you do not want to trust in Christ Jesus as your great Protector and Helper, Luke 14:32 suggests that a message be sent to the enemy, Satan, asking him for conditions of peace. There is absolutely nothing that you have to do, because Satan already is in control of your life. Christ wants us to know that the Christian life is one battle after another. **He wants us to trust Him completely.**

6. As a disciple of Christ, <u>do we have to forsake everything we have</u>? Many stumble over the passage in Luke 14:33, thinking that it is commanding us to forsake our earthly possessions. We need to recognize that we cannot trust in our possessions in order to receive salvation or favor with God. Jesus Christ spoke to the rich young ruler, declaring almost the same thing in Mark 10:17–23. Why was Jesus so drastic with him? Mark 10:24 shows us the reason. Christ Jesus knew the heart of this young man, and He also knows our heart. This young man had placed his "trust in riches." In other words, he loved his possessions instead of loving God above all things.

The Apostle Paul lived what Christ taught and he declared in Philippians 3:4–8: "Yea doubtless, and I count all things but _____ for the excellency of the knowledge of Christ Jesus my Lord: for whom I have suffered the loss of all things, and do count them but _____, that I may win (please) Christ." Neither the Apostle Paul, nor anyone else can win his salvation by what he can give or what he can do. God provided Paul's necessities as he mentions in Philippians 4:12: "I know both how to be _____, and I know how to abound: everywhere and in all things I am instructed both to be full and to be hungry, both to abound and to suffer need." The Apostle Paul had given himself totally to the Lord to be used as God desired. He had his heart open to God so that he could do His will. All that he had and did was for the honor and glory of Jesus Christ.

7. As a disciple of Christ, <u>we must be a genuine Christian and not just an imitation</u>.

The last teaching that Christ Jesus mentions in Luke 14:34 is regarding salt. Some substances can appear to be salt, but if it has no qualities of true salt, what good is it? It only has the appearance of salt, which is of no value. God wants us to be a genuine Christian and not just someone that appears to be a Christian. Many say they are Christians, when they really are not. Of what value is their profession? Verse 35 says, "It is neither _____ for the _____, nor yet for the _____." So Christ warns us about those that just make a "profession of faith." What good is this profession?_____ He finishes this passage by saying, "He that hath ears to hear, let him _____." It is indispensable for us to be true and authentic Christians. God knows the difference.

Summary:

All people without Christ are lost, and cannot save themselves. God loves us and did everything possible to save us: He sent His Son, Jesus Christ to this earth, placed all our sin upon Himself, received the wrath of God, and died in our place. Christ Jesus arose physically from the dead after three days and nights in the tomb. Our salvation depends completely upon this truth. Salvation is only received when we repent and trust with all our heart in Jesus Christ as our only sufficient Savior. This salvation does not depend upon our good works. Before we are saved, we are in a great battle against God and need to surrender to Him. We receive eternal life the moment that we trust in Christ, and we become sons of God.

REVIEW QUESTIONS

CHAPTER 5 — SALVATION: THE SPIRITUAL BIRTH

1. Why is salvation necessary? _____ _____
   _____

2. How did God show His love? (Romans 5:8)_____
   _____

3. How do we receive salvation? (Ephesians 2:8–9) _____
   _____

4. Is our repentance, for the sin we have committed, necessary for our salvation? _____

5. Is it possible for us to repent of our sin, place our complete faith in Christ with all our heart, and then guard it as a secret? _____

6. When you become a true Christian, is it possible that you will suffer persecution for your new life in Christ from family and friends? _____

7. Do you realize that you are a terrible sinner? _____

8. Are you trusting that Jesus Christ died on the cross and arose from the dead, completely paying the debt for your sin? _____

9. Are you truly repentant of all your sins, which are offenses against God and others? _____

10. Are you ready to give yourself with all your heart to Christ to become His property? _____ Do you want to do the will of God in your life? _____

If you have any doubts, you should study again the preceding chapters and talk with your counselor about your doubts.

God's plan of salvation is simple and easy to understand. With all sincerity pray to God, acknowledging that the Lord Jesus Christ died on the cross to pay the debt for your sin and physically arose from the dead to save you. Recognize your terrible, sinful condition and truly express repentance for your sin. As you pour out your heart to Him, ask for forgiveness for your sin. Ask Him to save you, trusting in the Lord Jesus Christ as your personal Savior. Give yourself to Jesus Christ, recognizing His authority over your life forever.

You can pray on your knees, standing or sitting. The position of the body is not important, but the condition of your heart is very important. **I trust that you will give yourself to Jesus Christ today.** *Please close the book, close your eyes in reverence to God and pour out your heart to Him.*

Did you give yourself to Jesus Christ, recognizing Him as your only sufficient Savior? _____ Did you repent of your sin and truly give yourself to Jesus Christ with all your heart? _____ Do you belong to Him? _____ Do you know for sure you are saved? _____ Are you saved for eternity or can you lose your salvation? _____

How do you know? Please study the following passages and choose a verse that clearly gives you assurance of salvation: John 1:12; Ephesians 2:1–5; 2 Timothy 1:12; Romans 8:16; 1 John 5:10–15; and Hebrews 7:25. Please write the verse here. _____

_____

_____

_____

If you have truly been converted to our Lord Jesus Christ, you should remember this important date.

_____	_____
My signature	Date

God has forgiven you and has received you into His family from the moment that you gave yourself to Jesus Christ. The Holy Spirit has come into your life to guide you. He has given you peace and joy that the world cannot give. You need to tell others of your conversion. God places a great responsibility on us to share our testimony with others regarding our salvation, so that they can also hear and believe.

It is good for you to give thanks to God and to Jesus Christ for your salvation. You can tell Him in prayer right now.

Please memorize Ephesians 2:8–9 and write it in your own words. _____

_____

_____

_____

———————————◆▸◆◂◆———————————

Please write and share your conversion with me, and any doubts that you might have regarding this lesson to the Bible Institute Correspondence Department: philippi@becoming-a-christian.org

The assurance of salvation does not come from yourself, from good feelings, or from your personal ideas, but from the Bible. Please continue studying the next lesson to understand more about the assurance of salvation for the true believer.

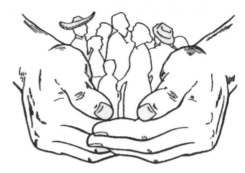

— Chapter Six —

The Security of the True Christian

My sheep hear my voice, and I know them, and they follow me: and I give unto
them eternal life; and they shall never perish, neither shall any man pluck them out of
my hand. My Father, which gave them me, is greater than all; and no man is able to
pluck them out of my Father's hand.

John 10:27–29

Yes, we can know that we are saved!

In 2 Timothy 1:12 the Apostle Paul declared: "I am not _____: for I know
whom I have believed, and am _____ that he is able to keep that which
I have committed unto him against that day." God in His infinite love and grace
has placed our guilt on Christ Jesus when He died on the cross for what our
sins deserved. Furthermore, Jesus Christ is seated in heaven as our mediator
before God the Father, so that we can receive His complete pardon.

Through the pardon of God, the guilt of sin has been removed, making it possible for man to be reconciled and established in harmony with God. All of
this came about when Jesus Christ our Savior made a covenant with the human
race, when He died on the cross. However, the only way that this covenant can
be effective is when the sinner repents of his sin and gives himself to Christ.
With complete clarity, the Bible teaches that the true believer can have the assurance of his salvation and eternal life, which comes only through the Word
of God, and not our feelings.

I. The assurance of GOD's forgiveness.

The Bible teaches us that true salvation comes directly from God. The
death, burial, and resurrection of Jesus Christ is God's provision to bring

about this eternal salvation. We cannot add anything to what the Lord Jesus Christ did for us in His perfect sacrifice on the cross. We reap the benefits of this provision when we repent of our sin, trust Christ as our Savior and give ourselves to Him.

1. The provision of forgiveness through Jesus Christ

    a. Christ Jesus gave His life and shed His blood on the cross for us. Ephesians 1:5–7 says, "Having predestinated us unto the _____ of children by Jesus Christ to himself, according to the good pleasure of his will, to the praise of the glory of his grace, wherein He hath made us accepted in the Beloved. In whom we have redemption through His _____, the forgiveness of sins, according to the riches of His grace."

    b. God put the conditions in order for us to receive His forgiveness. If we confess our sin with true repentance, there will be immediate pardon from God and communion will be established with Him. We should not try to defend our sinful actions. It is very important that we maintain our life transparent and not try to hide our sins. Proverbs 28:13–14 says, "He that covereth his sins shall not prosper: but whoso _____ and _____ them shall have mercy. Happy is the man that feareth alway: but he that hardeneth his heart shall fall into _____." Christ is our faithful and just Mediator before God to defend us, but He will not defend sin. According to 1 John 2:1, Christ presents Himself as our faithful and just lawyer before God. "And if any man sin, we have a _____ (Lawyer or go-between) with the Father, Jesus Christ the righteous." Jesus knows our problems and how to present our case before God, our Judge. He intercedes for us and we are forgiven (pardoned). Immediately our communication and communion is reestablished with our Father.

2. The promise of forgiveness by God

    a. God promises that He will be merciful to us if we will ask Him for forgiveness for our sin." Isaiah 55:7 insists, "Let the wicked forsake his way, and the unrighteous man his thoughts: and let him return unto the Lord, and He will have _____ upon him; and to our God, for He will abundantly _____." If there really is repentance

for our sin and confession of them **to Christ,** "He is _____ and
_____ to forgive us our sins, and to cleanse us from all unrighteousness." The word *confess* means — *to say the same thing or be
in agreement with.* In this case God wants us to recognize what we
have done wrong and agree with God. It is not just to admit that we
have done wrong, but to truly be repentant for our sins, recognizing
that we have offended God. Therefore, we have to confess our sin,
name them, and with repentance ask for forgiveness. This confession is done by means of direct prayer to God the moment we realize
that we have sinned.

b. What does God promise to do with our sin? Psalm 103:12 states,
"As far as the east is from the west, so far hath he _____ our
transgressions from us." Micah 7:19 also assures us that "He will
turn again, he will have compassion upon us; he will subdue our
iniquities; and thou wilt cast all their _____ into the depths of the
_____." In Hebrews 10:17 Christ promised: "And their _____
and iniquities will I _____ no more."

3. The results of confessing our sin

a. God hears us when we accept His conditions and respond with
obedience. We must obey quickly. 2 Chronicles 7:14–15 says, "If
my people, which are called by my name, shall _____ themselves, and pray, and seek my face, and _____ from their wicked
ways; then will I hear from heaven, and will forgive their sin, and
will heal their land. Now mine eyes shall be open, and mine ears at-
tent unto the prayer that is made in this place." God acts in love and
tenderness toward us, desiring the best for our lives.

b. God gives us joy and peace. Romans 15:13 declares, "Now the God
of hope fill you with all _____ and _____ in believing, that ye
may abound in hope, through the power of the Holy Ghost." After
confessing our sin, we have to escape from the things that Satan
wants to use to tempt us. In 2 Timothy 2:22, Paul warns Timothy:
"Flee also youthful lusts: but _____ righteousness, faith, charity
(love), peace, with them that call on the Lord out of a pure _____ ."
By doing this, He can bless us with His peace and joy.

c. Because we have become members of God's family, the blood of Jesus Christ is applied to each one of us and it is sufficient to cleanse us from all sin, past, present, and even those of the future. The Apostle John in 1 John 1:7, encourages us to maintain a true fellowship with Christ by saying, "But if we walk in the light, as he is in the light, we have _____ one with another, and the blood of Jesus Christ his Son cleanseth us from _____ sin."

4. The outcome of unconfessed sin

a. When we do not confess our sins, our fellowship with the Lord Jesus Christ is broken. We know that God always wants to have a loving relationship and fellowship with us. How could God have fellowship with our sins? _____ What happens if we do not confess our sins? _____ What does God say regarding the person who has the idea that he has not sinned? _____ _____ 1 John 1:8 declares: "If we say that we have no sin, we _____ ourselves, and the truth is not in us." We should not deny our sin but recognize what we have done and not wait until later to confess it. Again the Apostle John repeats in 1 John 1:10, "If we say that we have not sinned, we make him a _____, and his word is not in us." By denying our sin we are actually calling God a liar. That person is a liar, and God's word is not in him.

Sin cannot make us lose our salvation; but sin can separate us from fellowship with God, just like disobedience disrupts our fellowship with our natural parents. If we refuse to recognize and confess our sins we cannot enjoy the same relationship with God as previously experienced. God wants to see sincerity on our part, removing the sinful ways in our life. Paul calls upon each Christian in 2 Corinthians 7:1 to correct his life: "Let us cleanse ourselves from _____ filthiness of the _____ and _____, perfecting holiness in the fear of God."

b. Sin is always an offence against the very nature and person of God. As a result we can expect God's discipline, not His blessings. If we continue in our sin, we can expect that our Father, who loves us so much, will discipline us like any father disciplines a disobedient son. True love is manifested in discipline. Hebrews 12:5–11 assures us that the purpose of discipline is to bring us to obedience: "My son, despise not thou the chastening of the Lord, nor faint when thou art rebuked of him: For whom the Lord _____ he _____, and scourgeth every son whom he receiveth. If ye endure chastening, God dealeth with you as with _____; for what son is he whom the father chasteneth not? . . . Now no chastening for the present seemeth to be joyous, but grievous: nevertheless afterward it yieldeth the peaceable _____ of righteousness unto them which are exercised thereby." God wants us to hate sin as He hates sin, and He wants us to judge sin as He judges sin. We have to act drastically with our own sin and judge it before God judges it. The Apostle Paul gives the warning in 2 Corinthians 5:10, that one day we will give account to God for what we have done. "For we must _____ appear before the judgment seat of Christ; that every one may receive the things done in his body, according to that he hath done, whether it be _____ or _____." According to Romans 8:1, if our sins have not been confessed, is it possible for the true Christian to be condemned to the Lake of Fire?

_____

   c. The person who says that he is a member of the family of God and practices sin in his life is not truly of God. He is not saved! It is declared in 1 John 3:8, "He that committeth (practices) sin is of the devil."

II. The assurance of salvation

There are many who believe they are in the truth, when in reality they are in error. Lamentably, this is the worst type of deception one can experience. That lie only comes from Satan. One should not permit his thoughts to betray him, believing that he is saved, if in reality he is lost. The Bible teaches us that the security of true salvation comes from God and not of ourselves. Salvation is based upon the grace of God, which brings us to faith and confidence in Christ, not in our feelings and emotions. We must not be misguided in our thinking, believing that we have salvation if we really do not. Neither should we permit Satan to rob us of our security if we really have been converted to Jesus Christ and belong to Him.

   1. We can have the assurance of our salvation because of what God the Father has done.

a. God made us His children. 1 Peter 2:9–10 says, "But ye are a chosen generation, a royal priesthood, an holy nation, a _____ (acquired) people, that ye should shew forth the praises of him who hath called you out of darkness into his marvellous light; Which in time past were not a people, but are _____ the people of God: which had not obtained mercy, but now have obtained mercy." The Apostle Paul confirms in Philippians 3:20 that "For our _____ (citizenship) is in heaven; from whence also we look for the Savior, the Lord Jesus Christ." The plan of salvation begins with God and is finished by Him. It is His plan and He carried out that plan in order to save us. When a person repents of his sin, puts his faith in the Lord Jesus Christ, and gives himself to the Lord, he becomes a son of God. In the same way that I will always be the son of my parents, even so my relationship of being a son of God is forever. Because I was born into the family of God, I can never lose this relationship.

b. God gave us His righteousness. The Apostle Paul, in Romans 4:1–5, tells us how we *receive* Jesus Christ. Verse 3 asks the question to make us think. "For what saith the Scripture? Abraham believed God, and it was **counted** unto him for righteousness." The word *counted* is a term used in accounting; as an action that occurs when a transfer is made from one account to another. This transfer is from God's account to Abraham's account. In other words when Abraham trusted Christ as his personal Savior, he *received* to his account salvation, because by faith he was placed into the family of God. God places this same salvation to our account only when we give ourselves to the Lord Jesus Christ and trust in Him as our personal Savior. Have you *received* this salvation to your account? _____ Christ declared in John 1:12, "But as many as **received** him, to them gave he power to become the sons of God, even to them that believe on his name." We understand this action of *receiving* is to deposit our full confidence in Jesus Christ.

c. We are His for all eternity. The true Christian is safe in the hands of God. Many falsely teach that the Christian can lose the salvation that God has given to him. In the Gospel of John 10:27 it says, "My sheep _____ my voice, and I know them, and **they follow me**." If you are truly saved, you are one of His sheep, and you will hear His Word, and you will faithfully follow Him. John 10:28–29 confirms that the salvation that Jesus Christ gives us is eternal. "And I give unto them eternal life; and they shall _____ perish, neither shall any man pluck them out of my hand. My Father, which gave them me, is greater than all; and _____ man is able to pluck them out of my Father's hand." **We are eternally safe.** We have read various passages that assure us of salvation. I strongly urge you to memorize some of the passages that the Bible treats regarding our assurance.

2. We can have the assurance of our salvation because of what Christ Jesus has done.

   a. Our salvation was bought by Christ when He died on the cross, shedding His blood to pay for our punishment. After three days in the tomb Christ Jesus **physically** arose to assure us that He had done all that was necessary to provide for us eternal salvation. Besides what He has already done, is there something yet for God to do in order to save us? _____ Is there something else that we have to achieve in order for Him to save us? _____ I can only receive salvation through faith, being repentant for my sin, and giving myself to the Lord Jesus Christ with all my heart.

   b. When Jesus Christ was crucified, His blood had to be shed. Hebrews 9:22 gives the explanation: "And almost all things are by the law purged with blood; and without shedding of blood is no _____ (forgiveness)." This is taught throughout the Old Testament Law. 1 Peter 3:18 gives a concise explanation why Jesus had to die: "For Christ also hath once suffered for sins, the just for the unjust, that he might _____ us to God, being put to death in the flesh, but _____ (made alive) by the Spirit." Lamentably there are religious people who try to achieve forgiveness through religious rites and traditions that do not serve. Hebrews 10:11 reminds us that "Every priest standeth daily ministering and offering oftentimes the same sacrifices, which can _____ take away sins." Hebrews 10:12 tells us that only one sacrifice is valid: "But this man (Jesus Christ), after he had offered _____ sacrifice for sins forever, _____ down on the right hand of God." Time after time the Bible reminds us that Jesus Christ finished His work so that it would never have to be repeated. Upon reading Hebrews 9:12; 9:25–28 and 10:10–14, it is clear that the ceremony of the *Sacrifice of the Mass* is anti-Biblical. Hebrews 10:10 affirms, "By the which will we are sanctified through the offering of the body of Jesus Christ _____ for all." A symbolic sacrifice is **never** to be offered, for it would be an act contrary to God's Word.

3. We can have the assurance of our salvation because of what the Holy Spirit has done.

    a. The moment that we gave ourselves to Jesus Christ, the Holy Spirit baptized us into God's family. 1 Corinthians 12:13 says, "For by one Spirit are we all _____ into one body." The word *baptism* means – *placed into*. We have been *placed into* the family of God by the work of God. All who have placed their confidence in Jesus Christ as their Savior have been *placed into the body of Christ*, which is His church. The baptism of the Holy Spirit is the act of placing the true believer into the family of God. This is explained in Ephesians 4:4–6 speaking of *one baptism* in the family of God. In this passage, *baptism* is not in water, but the placement of the true Christian into the family of God forever.

    b. From the moment we gave ourselves to Jesus Christ, the Holy Spirit entered our life, and put upon us His *seal* of ownership. Paul confirms in 2 Corinthians 3:3–4: "Forasmuch as ye are manifestly declared to be the epistle of Christ ministered by us, written not with _____, but with the _____ of the living God; not in tables of stone, but in fleshy tables of the _____. And such trust have we through Christ to God-ward." Ephesians 1:13 tells us when we were sealed: "In whom ye also trusted, after that ye heard the word of truth, the gospel of your salvation: in whom also after that ye _____, ye were _____ with that Holy Spirit of promise." Why is this important? Ephesians 1:14 continues, "Which is the earnest (the assurance or down payment) of our _____ until the redemption of the purchased possession, unto the praise of His glory." If we make a contract to purchase a property, a deed is made. Both sign it and an official seal is placed on it. From this moment the buyer has the **assurance** that this is his property. We who have the seal of the Holy Spirit upon our life can be sure that God will finish the work that He has started. Philippians 1:6 assures us by saying: "Being _____ of this very thing, that he which hath begun a good work in you will perform it until the day of Jesus Christ." We are His forever.

c. The Holy Spirit lives in every Christian from the moment that he trusts in Christ as his Savior. The Holy Spirit does not come into us little by little. We do not receive our salvation first and the Holy Spirit afterwards. Jesus Christ clarifies this in John 3:34 saying, "For God giveth not the Spirit by _____ unto him." Jesus again declares in John 14:17, "Even the Spirit of truth; whom the world cannot receive, because it seeth him not, neither knoweth him: but ye know him; for he ___ _____ with you, and shall be _____ you." If you have put your trust in Christ as your Savior, the Holy Spirit lives in you! Does the Holy Spirit live in you? _____ What should we say about a Christian that sins? Can a true Christian lose his salvation? In the light of God's Word, the true Christian **does not lose his salvation** because he has sinned, but the Holy Spirit brings conviction of the sin and He brings us to repentance and confession of sin, asking forgiveness from God. If you have not trusted Christ as your Savior, sin will not disturb you and you will continue to sin. Romans 8:9 warns, "if any man have not the _____ of Christ, he is _____ of his."

4. We can have the assurance of our salvation because of what the Bible promises.

a. The Apostle Paul had this great assurance and gave testimony of it in 2 Timothy 1:12: "For the which cause I also suffer these things: nevertheless I am not ashamed: for I _____ whom I have believed, and am persuaded that he is able to _____ that which I have committed unto him against that day." God desires for us to **know for sure** we are saved and to whom we belong. To whom do you belong? _____

b. The Bible is full of promises of assurance of salvation for the true Christian. John 5:24 gives us another confirmation of our salvation: "He that heareth my word, and believeth on Him that sent me, hath _____ life, and shall not come into condemnation; but is passed from death unto _____."

73

c. God guides His children. Romans 8:14 declares, "For as many as are _____ by the Spirit of God, they are the sons of God." We should desire to be continually led by God through the teaching of His Word; therefore we should be faithful in the study of the Bible.

d. Read 1 John 5:10. "He that believeth (deposits his trust) on the Son of God hath the _____ in himself." The *witness,* who is referred to here, is the Spirit of God, who came to dwell in us when we gave ourselves to Christ! Romans 8:16 explains, "The Spirit itself beareth _____ with our spirit, that we are the _____ of God." The true Christian knows in his heart that he is a son of God. In 1 John 5:11–13 the Apostle John declared, "And this is the record, that God hath given to us eternal _____, and this _____ is in his Son. He that hath the Son hath _____; and he that hath not the Son of God hath not life. These things have I written unto you that believe (to deposit our complete confidence) on the name of the Son of God; that ye may _____ that ye have eternal life, and that ye may believe on the name of the Son of God." When it speaks of His *name,* it refers to all that is represented by the name of the Son of God: for what He is, and for what He has done for us when He died and arose from the dead to save us. God wants us to **know** that we belong to Him. Are you sure that you are a child of God? _____

III. The results of salvation

When a person has given himself by faith to Christ, God produces many changes in his life. Some of these changes are:

1. You have a new birth.

Christ Jesus declares in John 3:3, "Verily, verily, I say unto thee, except a man be born _____, he cannot see the kingdom of God." God's Word confirms this spiritual birth in 1 Peter 1:23 by saying: "Being born again, not of _____ seed, but of incorruptible, by the _____ of God, which liveth and abideth forever." How is this change accomplished? Again, God explains it in Ezekiel 36:26–27: "A _____ heart also will I give you, and a new _____ will I put within you: and I will take away the _____ heart out of your flesh, and I will give you an heart of flesh. And I will put my _____ within you, and cause you to walk in my _____, and ye shall keep my judgments, and _____ them." What a blessing!

74

2. You have a new life.

   In 1 John 5:12 the Apostle John gives assurance to the new believer: "He that hath the _____ hath _____; and he that hath not the Son of God hath not life." In 2 Corinthian 5:17, the Apostle Paul gives three biblical truths that sum up the changes in your life: "Therefore if any man be in Christ, he is a _____ creature: _____ things are passed away; behold, all things are become _____." Jesus Christ makes a transformation in the life of those who place their confidence in Him. In verse 18 it declares that "all things are of _____." Only God can do this in your life. 1 Peter 2:2 instructs those who are born again, "As newborn babes, desire the sincere milk of the _____, that ye may grow thereby." What happens if someone does not desire to receive this spiritual food? It is sad, because it shows that he does not love God, nor is there a desire to have fellowship with Him.

3. You have a new family.

   In Christ we became part of a new family. Now we can exclaim, "I am one of God's children and I know that I belong to Him!" John 1:12 says, "But as many as received him, to them gave he power to become the _____ of God, even to them that believe on his name." God has made me a member of His family! God is my Father, and the other believers who have come to know the Lord Jesus Christ as their Savior are my new brothers and sisters. We recognize other believers as *brethren in the faith* because we really are members of the same family. This is confirmed in Hebrews 2:11, "For both He that sanctifieth (Christ Jesus) and they who are sanctified are all of one: for which cause he is not ashamed to call them _____." Ephesians 2:19 also confirms this relationship: "Now therefore ye are no more strangers and foreigners, but fellow-citizens with the saints, and of the _____ of God." Truly, we are of the family of God! 1 John 3:1–2 exclaims, "Behold, what manner of love the Father hath bestowed upon us, that we should be called the sons of God: therefore the world knoweth us not, because it knew him not. Beloved, now are we the _____ of God…"

4. You have a new relationship.
   a. We are God's friends! When we trust in Christ as our personal Savior, God gives us a new relationship. Jesus Christ expressed this as-

sociation in John 15:15, "Henceforth I call you not _____; for the servant knoweth not what his lord doeth: but I have called you _____; for all things that I have heard of my Father I have made known unto you." Colossians 1:21 says that we have the presence of Christ in our life. What were the two conditions in the past that showed that we were removed from God? _____ and _____. Before we lived in disobedience to God, but when we trusted Christ as our Savior, we gained a new relationship.

b. We are His adopted sons and therefore heirs of God's possessions. The following passages confirm this important relationship in the family of God: 2 Corinthians 6:17–18 declares, "... I will receive you. And will be a Father unto you, and ye shall be my _____ and _____, saith the Lord Almighty." Romans 8:16–17 says, "The Spirit himself beareth witness with our spirit, that we are the children of God: And if children, then _____; heirs of God, and joint-heirs with Christ; if so be that we suffer with him, that we may be also glorified together."

c. We are servants of Jesus Christ. The Apostle Paul considered it a great privilege to be a servant of Jesus Christ and of all the brethren. He declared it repeatedly throughout his writings. In 2 Corinthians 4:5 he mentions, "For we preach not ourselves, but Christ Jesus the Lord; and ourselves your _____ for Jesus' sake."

5. You have a new name.

Ephesians 3:14–15 says: "For this cause I bow my knees unto the _____ of our Lord Jesus Christ, of whom the whole family in heaven and earth is _____." God is Holy, and we who are true Christians are holy. Maybe you have never considered yourself to be a *saint*. It is possible that you have a wrong concept like many other people have regarding the meaning of *saint*. The word *saint* means – *separated*. In the Biblical use of the word, it is to be *separated from the world for the use of God*. Christ has declared us *righteous* before God and has made us *saints*. God is changing us day by day. We see the reconciling work of Christ in Colossians 1:22; "to present you _____ and unblamable and _____ in His sight." The Apostle Paul introduces his first letter to the church of Corinth saying in 1 Corinthians 1:2, "Unto the church of God which is at Corinth, to them that are _____ in Christ Jesus, called to be _____, with all that in every place call upon the name of Jesus Christ our Lord, both theirs and _____." God wants us to remember that we belong to Him, and that we are to serve Him. He is our owner, and we are His possession.

6. You have new responsibilities.

God desires that we live to please Him in all that we do without sin, but since it is impossible, God has made a provision for us. The forgiveness of God toward us is great and complete; and it is indispensable if we are to have fellowship with Him. Jesus Christ wants to cleanse us from sin, as 1 John 1:9 affirms, "If we confess our sins, he is faithful and just to forgive us our sins, and to _____ us from all unrighteous- ness." After saving us, God wants to see action on our part. He tells us to clean up things in our life that are in direct opposition to our new God-given nature. Paul writes in 2 Corinthians 7:1, "Having therefore these promises, dearly beloved, let us cleanse ourselves from all filthi- ness of the _____ and _____, perfecting holiness in the fear of God." God does not give us any options. It is extremely important to maintain our life transparent and not hold on to sin. We should never try to hide our sin, but to confess it to Christ. Proverbs 28:13 warns, "He that covereth his sins shall not prosper: but whoso _____ and _____ them shall have _____."

7. You have a new love.

There are no limits to our love, because God has given us His complete love! Romans 5:5 helps us to understand that "the _____ of God is shed abroad in our _____ by the Holy Spirit which is given unto us." The love of God never ends. One of the most convincing evidences that a person has eternal life in Christ Jesus is the love of God being manifested in his life. When our heart has been changed, God will also transform our mentality. The former hostility that we had will be sub- stituted by a true and holy love. Jesus Christ declared in Mark 12:30–31 that the first and great commandment is: "And thou shalt _____ the Lord thy God with all thy heart, and with all thy soul, and with all thy mind, and with all thy strength: this is the first commandment. And the second is like, namely this, Thou shalt _____ thy neighbor as thyself." An intense love for God and others exists in the deepest senti- ments of the regenerated heart!

The Apostle John could talk with authority, because he repeated the Words of Christ when he said in John 13:34: "A new commandment I give unto you, that ye _____ one another; as I have _____ you, that ye also _____ one another." The Lord Jesus Christ commands that **we love as He loves**. It is not only saying that we love one another, but that we love in truth and in our deeds. In the family of God, the son is not only loved by the Father, but also by the brethren. No one realized this love as much as the beloved Apostle John. He firmly declares in 1 John 3:14: "We know that we have passed from death unto life, because we _____ the _____. He that _____ not his brother abideth in death." The Apostle John admonishes us in 1 John 3:18: "My little children, let us not _____ in **word**, neither in <u>tongue</u>; but in _____ and in **truth**." It is impossible to give too much emphasis to this. John even declares in 1 John 4:7–8, 11–12: "Beloved, let us _____ one another: for love is of God; and every one that loveth is born of God, and knoweth God. He that loveth not knoweth not God; for God is love… beloved, if God so loved us, we ought also to love one another. No man hath seen God at any time. If we love one another, God dwelleth in us, and his _____ is perfected in us." Do you love others in this manner? _____

8. You have new desires, new activities, new attitudes and new goals. God gives us an order in 1 Peter 1:14–16 that we not only have the name *holy*, but that we must be in obedience to God: "As obedient children, not fashioning yourselves according to the former _____ in your ignorance: But as he which hath called you is holy, so be ye _____ in _____ manner of conversation; because it is written, be ye holy; for I am holy." Ephesians 2:1–3 refers to our former life, but in verses 4 and 5 it confirms: "But God, who is rich in mercy, for his great love wherewith he loved us, even when we were _____ in sins, hath quickened (given life to) us together with Christ, (by grace ye are saved.)" This happened instantly the moment of our new birth. Now that we are God's children, He changes our old nature continually to be conformed to His nature. Sin does not produce the satisfaction it did before; to the contrary, it makes us feel sad. You will find that the things you did before are no longer *fun* and *attractive*. Things are different now! Why are these changes happening? Ephesians 2:10 responds, "For we are his workmanship, _____ in Christ Jesus unto good

works, which God hath before ordained that we should _____ in them." The reason is that we have a new life in Christ Jesus. Now we belong to Christ and not to the world.

God expects this change to be visible in your life, to you and to others. He expects our actions to be in accord with our identification with Christ. It is not just a fact that we are *born again*, but we also must have a normal development in our new life. It is a command from God in 2 Peter 3:18, "But _____ in grace, and in the knowledge of our Lord and Savior Jesus Christ." In order to grow it is necessary to daily feed upon the Word of God. Not only should you study and meditate in the Bible, but also it is indispensable to attend worship services where sound doctrine in the Word of God is being preached. This is extremely important.

We want to follow Him, as Jesus describes in John 10:27: "My sheep hear my voice, and I know them, and they _____ me." Our conduct must express the life that we now have in Christ. 1 John 2:6 tell us, "He that saith he abideth in ____ ought himself also so to walk, even as _____ walked." The Apostle Paul gives us the command in Romans 12:2, "Be _____ conformed to this world: but be ye _____ by the renewing of your _____, that ye may prove what is that good, and acceptable, and perfect, will of God." Romans 8:9 reminds us that He lives in us: "But ye are not in the _____, (living according to fleshly desires) but in the _____, if so be that the Spirit of God dwell in you. Now if any man have not the Spirit of Christ, he is none of his." Is it your desire to separate yourself from a worldly life and live for Jesus Christ? _____

True believers desire that others come to know the Lord Jesus Christ as their personal Savior. Do you want to tell the world that you now belong to the Lord Jesus Christ? _____ There are many changes in our attitudes that God gives to the believers. In Romans 1:16 the Apostle declared, "For I am not _____ of the gospel of Christ: for it is the power of God unto salvation to every one that believeth; to the Jew first, and also to the Greek." Now we are not ashamed to talk with others and share with them our testimony about our conversion to Jesus Christ.

9. You have a new hope.

In John 14:1–3, Christ speaks of a great hope: "Let not your heart be troubled: ye believe in God, believe also in me. In my Father's house are many _____: if it were not so, I would have told you. I go to prepare a _____ for you. And if I go and prepare a place for you, I will come again, and _____ you unto myself; that where I am, there ye may be also." This teaching about the reality of the return of the Lord Jesus Christ for His own is referred to as the *rapture*. It is confirmed and explained by the Apostle Paul when he wrote 1 Thessalonians 4:13–18. In verse 17 it says, "Then we which are alive and remain shall be _____ together with them in the clouds, to meet the _____ in the air: and so shall we ever be with the Lord." This is the glorious hope and security of the Christian! We will have transformed bodies and will physically be present with Jesus Christ forever. In 1 Corinthians 2:9 Paul exclaimed: "Eye hath not seen, nor ear heard, neither have entered into the _____ of man, the things which God hath _____ for them that love him."

10. We have a personal teacher, the Holy Spirit.

The Apostle Paul explains the ministry of the Holy Spirit in 1 Corinthians 2:12–13; "Now we have received, not the spirit of the world, but the _____ which is of God; that we might know the things that are freely given to us of God. Which things also we speak, not in the words which man's wisdom teacheth, but which the Holy Ghost _____; comparing spiritual things with spiritual." This means that the Holy Spirit helps us to understand the spiritual teaching by comparing the teaching in one passage of God's Word with other passages.

Summary:

What are the results of salvation in your life? God brings many changes into the life of the new believer. He has new life and belongs to a new family. He has new desires, new attitudes, new actions and new purposes. The Christian also has the new responsibilities to grow in the grace and knowledge of our Lord and Savior Jesus Christ and at the same time live a holy life. If we confess our sins we can **know** that God has forgiven us all the sins of our past life.

We can also **know** that we are saved and maintained by God's hands, which will not let us fall. The Apostle Paul expressed his relationship with Christ in Galatians 2:20 saying: "I am crucified with _____: nevertheless I live; yet not I, but Christ liveth in me: and the life which I now live in the flesh I live by the faith of the Son of God, who loved me, and gave himself for _____."
We cannot do anything to help Christ save us. As repentant sinners we can only surrender to Him with all our heart. The Apostle Paul explains, in Galatians 3:15, a great truth on assurance: "Though it be but a man's covenant, yet if it be confirmed, no man disannulleth (to cancel), or _____ thereto." No one can better, or add to the true work of God.

REVIEW QUESTIONS
CHAPTER 6 — THE ASSURANCE OF THE TRUE CHRISTIAN

1. Why did Jesus Christ die? (1 Peter 3:18) _____
_____

2. Are you sure that Jesus Christ has saved you? _____

3. How do you know that you have the security of your salvation? _____ _
_____

4. Upon what Bible verses can you base the assurance of your salvation?
_____

5. Will you go to heaven when you die to spend all eternity with God? _____
How do you know? _____

6. What is a saint? _____

7. How are we sanctified? (Hebrews 10:10) "By the which will we are sanctified through the offering of the body of Jesus Christ _____ for _____ (for all eternity)."

8. Do you still sin at times? _____

9. What things can separate us from the love of Christ? (Romans 8:35–39)
_____

10. What can break our <u>relationship with God</u> as His sons? _____

_____

11. What things can break our <u>fellowship with God</u> as His sons? _____

_____

12. Which sin can cause us to lose our salvation? _____

13. If we have repented of our sin, is there a sin too terrible from our past that God cannot forgive? _____

14. Is there some penitence (special payment) that you have to do to satisfy God so that He will forgive you? _____ What? _____

15. How many times does Jesus have to die as a sacrifice for our sins? _____

_____

16. Does there exist some ceremony, such as *the sacrifice of the mass*, which can bring you grace, or help you be more spiritual, or make possible your communion with God? _____ Why? _____

17. Why was it necessary for Jesus Christ to shed His blood on the cross and not just die in some other manner? (Hebrews 9:22) _____

_____

18. According to Proverbs 28:13, what two things should a believer do when he sins? _____

19. When a Christian has sinned, but does not want to recognize it, much less confess it, nor ask forgiveness from God, what will happen? (Hebrews 12:5–11) _____ For what purpose does God apply discipline? _____

20. In John 10:27–28, to whom is the Shepherd referring? _____
To whom do the sheep refer? _____

21. What does Christ promise in John 10:28? _____

_____

22. What does Christ promise in John 10:29? _____

_____

23. When the believer is at the Judgment Seat of Christ, will he give an account of himself? _____ According to 2 Corinthians 5:10, regarding what things will he give an account? _____ Is it possible for the true believer to be sent to eternal condemnation? _____

Please memorize John 10:27–29 and express it in your own words. _____

_____

_____

_____

_____

Please send your answers to the questions and any doubts that you might have regarding this lesson to the Bible Institute Correspondence Department: philippi@becoming-a-christian.org

Why do some Christians overcome sin and others fail? The next chapter will help you.

— Chapter Seven —

Power to Overcome Temptations and Trials

There hath no temptation taken you but such as is common to man:
but God is faithful, who will not suffer you to be tempted above that ye are able;
but will with the temptation also make a way to escape,
that ye may be able to bear it. 1 Corinthians 10:13

When we become a true Christian, we enter a battlefield.

God wants us to know that daily battles will confront us in the Christian life. In 1 Peter 5:8–9 the Apostle Peter warns: "Be sober, be vigilant; because **your adversary the devil**, as a roaring _____, walketh about, seeking whom he may devour: Whom _____ stedfast in the faith, knowing that the same afflictions are accomplished in your brethren that are in the _____." The Apostle Paul warned his coworker, Timothy, of many dangers. In 2 Timothy 2:3–4 he said, "Thou therefore endure hardness, as a _____ soldier of Jesus Christ. No man that warreth entangleth himself with the affairs of this life; that he may please Him who hath chosen him to be a _____." God has called us to a life of discipline, separation and holiness, not to a worldly life.

It is not a normal battle or a normal battlefield. Here the enemy attacks from all sides and from within a church or congregation. We see an illustration of this attack through an experience in the life of Peter in Matthew 16:21–23: "From that time forth began Jesus to shew unto his disciples, how that he must go unto Jerusalem, and suffer many things of the elders and chief priests and scribes, and be killed, and be raised again the third day. Then Peter took him, and began to rebuke him, saying, be it far from thee, Lord: this shall not be unto thee. But he turned, and said unto Peter, Get thee behind me, _____: thou art an offence unto me: for thou savourest (comprehend) not the things that be of God, but those that be of men." In Ephesians 6:12 we read, "For we _____ not against flesh and blood, but against principalities, against powers, against the rulers of the _____ of this world, against spiritual _____ in high places."

Our enemies cannot be entirely eliminated or destroyed. **This is a lifelong battle.** Our victories are from moment to moment and from day to day. Only when the Lord Jesus Christ comes to take us home to be with Him will we experience complete victory. We have to trust Jesus Christ, and give thanks for every victory, as the Apostle Paul confidently expressed in 1 Corinthians 15:57: "But thanks be to God, which giveth us the _____ through our Lord Jesus Christ."

I. There are three principal enemies of the Christian: the world, the flesh and the devil.

The Bible teaches us that these enemies attack the Christian from three different directions to provoke us to sin. The Christian is tempted to sin for three different reasons:

1. The world tempts us to sin.

   a. The Christian lives in a perverse and sinful world that deceives and attacks the believer when he least expects. The Bible makes reference to these things in many parts. The attack on the believer's life is an attraction for material things. Almost all evil is related to and rotating around money. The Apostle Paul carefully gives his counsel to his fellow partner in 1 Timothy 6:9–10: "But they that will be _____ fall into temptation and a snare, and into many foolish and hurtful lusts, which _____ men in destruction and perdition. For the _____ of money is the root of all evil: which while some coveted after, they have erred from the faith, and pierced themselves through with many _____." The worldly attractions; prestige, financial success, materialism, vices, sinful habits, vile worldly entertainments, and material gains are powerful temptations. All these things try to invade the life of the Christian. What command does God give to the Christian as to

86

worldly things? According to 1 John 2:15–16, "_____ not the _____, neither the things that are in the _____." It continues telling us the reason why we cannot love those things. "If any man _____the world, the _____ of the Father is not in him." The *world* refers to the sinful system that strips our love for God. James 4:4 teaches that "The friendship of the world is _____ with God."

b. Any person that can love and participate in worldly things, and at the same time believe that he is God's property is deceiving himself. We cannot deceive God. 1 John 2:3–4 identifies the person that pretends to be a child of God, but does not obey His Word: "Hereby we do know that we know him, if we keep his commandments. He that saith, I know him, and keepeth not his commandments, is a _____, and the truth is not in him." Again he states in 1 John 3:8, "He that committeth (practices) sin is of the __ _____." 1 John 3:9 presents the positive side: "Whosoever is born of God doth not _____ (practice) sin; for his seed remaineth in him: and he cannot sin, because he is _____ of God." God's desire is that we live a life pleasing to Him, without sin. Because this is impossible, God has made provision for us when we sin. God compels us to repent and confess our sin and return to have intimate fellowship with Him.

c. There are oppositions that can discourage the believer. In Luke 12:51, Jesus predicted difficult oppositions from family members saying: "Suppose ye that I am come to give _____ on earth? I tell you, Nay; but rather _____: For from henceforth there shall be five in one house _____, three against two, and two against three. The father shall be _____ against the son, and the son against the father; the mother against the daughter, and the daughter against the mother; the mother-in-law against her daughter-in-law, and the daughter-in-law against her mother-in-law." Families turn against one of their own members because they do not like the change that their new faith in Christ has brought into their lives. They see it as a threat to their religion and way of life.

2. The flesh tempts us to sin.

a. When we give ourselves to Christ, we receive a new nature that comes

87

from God; however, we will always have our human sinful nature. (The Bible refers to this sinful nature as the *flesh*.) Paul mentions a great conflict between the two natures of the believer in Galatians 5:17: "For the flesh lusteth _____ the Spirit, and the Spirit _____ the flesh: and these are contrary the one to the other: so that ye cannot do the things that ye would." There exists this conflict to some degree in us all. If we act in the flesh, we are our own worst enemy! Many activities related to the old nature are mentioned in Galatians 5:19–21, which terminates with, "they which do such things shall ____ inherit the kingdom of God." The characteristics of the new life are mentioned in Galatians 5:22–25, finishing with, "If we live in the Spirit, let us also _____ in the Spirit."

b. Being that there is so much wickedness in the heart of men, the Apostle Paul warned Timothy in 2 Timothy 3:1–7 saying, "This know also, that in the last days perilous times shall come. For men shall be _____ of their own selves, covetous, boasters, proud, blasphemers, _____ to parents, unthankful, unholy, without natural affection, trucebreakers, false accusers, incontinent, fierce, _____ of those that are _____, traitors, heady, highminded, lovers of pleasures more than lovers of God; having a _____ of godliness, but denying the power thereof: from such turn away. For of this sort are they which creep into houses, and lead captive silly women laden with _____, led away with divers lusts, ever learning, and never able to come to the knowledge of the truth."

c. The Apostle Paul clearly teaches what God expects us to do regarding our former way of life. It is indispensable for us to recognize our problem and drastically care for it. We cannot be friendly with the enemies of our soul, thinking they will leave us on their own. Colossians 3:5–7 ordered us to, "_____ (make die) therefore your members which are upon the earth (the worldly life); fornication, uncleanness, inordinate affection, evil concupiscence, and covetousness, which is idolatry: For which things' sake the wrath of God cometh on the children of disobedience: In the which ye also _____ some time, when ye lived in them." The phrase *mortify therefore your members*, has reference to a constant effort of putting sin to death. It does not happen once for all, but is a continual action.

We must decide to put an end to the worldliness in our life, since it is an enemy of God. Many times people blame the devil for the problems in their life, when in reality it is a result of their own sinful *fleshly* desires." The Apostle Paul forcefully insists in Ephesians 4:22: "That ye put off concerning the former conversation (manner of life) the old man, which is corrupt according to the _____ _____ lusts." Are you having discouragements and defeats in your life? Examine carefully your heart and look for the solution according to God's Word, and then take necessary measures to make the corrections.

3. The devil tempts us to sin.

   a. The devil is our major enemy. Satan wants to trip us and make us fall, and for this reason the Apostle Paul insisted that we know his tactics. 2 Corinthians 2:11 warns, "Lest Satan should get an advantage of us: for we are not _____ of his _____." For our own protection, we have to be careful to obey the command that Paul gave in Ephesians 4:27 saying, "Neither give _____ to the devil." We should not try to combat him; therefore we need to leave him. On one occasion, the Apostle Peter fell into Satan's trap. He expressed his own desires and worldly feelings, and as a result the Lord Jesus Christ strongly reprehended him in Matthew 16:21–23, "But he turned, and said unto Peter, Get thee behind me, Satan: thou art an _____ unto me: for thou savourest not the things that be of God, but those that be of men."

   b. Satan transforms himself into an *angel of light* with the purpose of deceiving us. The Apostle Paul declares in 2 Corinthians 11:13–14, "For such are false apostles, deceitful workers, transforming themselves into the apostles of Christ. And no marvel; for _____ himself is **transformed** into an _____ ____ of light." Satan wants to deceive us, mislead us, and discourage us by putting snares in our path. Eve listened to him and was deceived. Paul shows his concern in 2 Corinthians 11:3 saying, "But I fear, lest by any means, as the _____ beguiled Eve through his _____ _____, **so your minds should be corrupted** from the simplicity that is in Christ." Satan attacks the senses and destroys our capacity to reason; it may be in the form of a person, music, entertainment, or other activities.

c. Satan is in control of this present age, and he continues to blind men's eyes so that they cannot see the truth of God's Word and believe. He does not want us to hear the Word, repent of our sin, or give ourselves to Jesus Christ as our Savior to be saved. God's Word tells us in 2 Corinthians 4:4, "In whom the _____ of this world (Satan) hath _____ the minds of them which believe not, lest the light of the glorious gospel of Christ, who is the image of God, should shine unto them."

II. How to have victory over our enemies.

1. We have to trust God.

   a. God provides all the necessary resources in order to have victory in our lives. He promises us in Hebrews 2:18, "For in that he himself hath suffered being _____, he is able to succor (give help) them that are _____." We must always remember the teachings of Paul in 2 Thessalonians 3:3: "But the Lord is _____, who shall stablish you, and _____ you from evil."

   b. If you willfully go against Him, God cannot protect you. It is always our personal responsibility to submit to God. Only in this way will we have the strength to resist the devil. James 4:7–8 commands, "_____ yourselves therefore to God. _____ the devil, and he will flee from you. _____ nigh to God, and he will draw nigh to you. _____ your hands, ye sinners; and purify your hearts, ye double minded."

   c. God provides the necessary resources for us to have victory in our life. The help exists for every situation and every circumstance to overcome temptations. Our memory verse, 1 Corinthians 10:13, is promising us, "...God is faithful, who will not suffer you to be tempted above that ye are _____; but will with the temptation also make a way to _____, that ye may be able to _____ it." God is faithful to guard us from the temptations that we are not able to resist. He will not leave us defenseless. In 2 Peter 2:9 the Apostle Peter wrote: "The Lord knoweth how to deliver the godly (the true Christian) out of _____, and to reserve the unjust unto the day of judgment to be punished." The Apostle Paul expressed gratitude in 2 Corinthians 2:14, "Now thanks be unto God, which always causeth us to _____ in Christ."

90

2. We have to be fortified by the Word of God.

   a. It is indispensable for us to **read** God's Word in order to have victory over the temptations that come our way." The Apostle John writes in 1 John 2:14: "I have written unto you, fathers, because ye have known him that is from the beginning. I have written unto you, young men, because ye are strong, and the word of God _____ (lives) in you, and ye have _____ the wicked one."

   b. It is indispensable for us to **meditate** on God's Word to have victory over temptations that come our way. God exhorts us in Deuteronomy 6:6–7: "And these words, which I command thee this day, shall be in thine heart: And thou shalt _____ them diligently unto thy children, and shalt _____ of them when thou _____ in thine house, and when thou _____ by the way, and when thou liest down, and when thou risest up." God commanded in Joshua 1: 8: "This book of the law shall not depart out of thy mouth; but thou shalt _____ therein day and night, that thou mayest observe to _____ according to all that is written therein: for then thou shalt make thy way prosperous, and then thou shalt have good success."

   c. It is indispensable for us to **memorize** key verses in God's Word to have victory over the temptations that come our way. King David expressed, in Psalm 119:11, the desire of his life: "Thy word have I _____ in mine _____, that I might not sin against thee." Why is it important to memorize God's Word? _____

   _____

3. We have to watch and pray.

   a. This is not a suggestion, but our responsibility to *watch*, being alert as soldiers, because we are in a war. In Matthew 26:41 Jesus Christ warns us to, "_____ and pray, that ye enter not into _____: the spirit indeed is _____, but the flesh is _____."

   b. The Apostle Paul is praying for the believers in Colossians 1:9–10, "For this cause we also, since the day we heard it, do not cease to _____ for you, and to desire that ye might be filled with the knowledge of his will in all wisdom and spiritual understanding; that ye might walk _____ of the Lord unto all pleasing, being fruitful in every good work, and increasing in the knowledge of God." Being tempted is not a sin in itself; however, when we yield to temptation that is sin. Ephesians 6:10–18 gives us a list of what to do to prepare against the attacks of Satan and "the rulers of darkness." Verse 18 admonishes us: "Praying always with all _____ and supplication in the Spirit, and _____ thereunto with all perseverance and supplication for all saints." We need to **pray** for strength and wisdom.

4. We have to recognize our sin, confess our sin, and ask forgiveness for our sin.

   a. We cannot ignore sin in our life. When we have sinned we must be quick to humble ourselves and recognize our sins. 1 John 1:8 warns, "If we say that we have no _____, we deceive ourselves, and the truth is not in us." Doing so we will only deceive ourselves, because no one can deceive God.

   b. Confession means – *to say the same thing, or be in agreement with*, and in this case it talks about being in agreement with God regarding our own sin. God wants us to agree with Him regarding what He says about our sins. It is not just admitting that we have done something wrong, but to truly repent of our sin and recognize how we have offended God. We must confess our sins to God immediately upon realizing that we have sinned against Him or others. What promise does Jesus Christ give us if we confess our sins to Him? It clearly affirms in 1 John 1:9: "If we confess our sins, he is faithful and just to _____ us our sins, and to _____ us from all unrighteousness." As soon as possible after realizing that we have sinned, we must humble ourselves and confess our sins to God.

5. We must recognize our weaknesses and that we cannot overcome them without God's help.

   a. On occasions we can overcome temptations and trials by our own strength; however, most of the time we will fail. Satan, our enemy, desires us to think that we are able to do it without God's help. 1 Corinthians 10:12 says, "Wherefore let him that _____ he standeth take _____ lest he fall." In Christ Jesus we have the assurance of victory because He dwells in us.

   b. God assures us, in 1 John 4:4, that we have God's help: "Ye are of

God, little children, and have _____ them: because greater is he that is in you, than he that is in the world." Romans 8:31 teaches that if we put Him first in our life, God will be in charge, and will help us: "What shall we then say to these things? If God be for us, who can be _____ us?" Here is the important question! Is God in favor of what you are doing and the manner in which you are living? _____ The testimony, given in Romans 8:35–39 by the Apostle Paul, has encouraged many Christians: "Nay, in all these things we are more than _____ through him that loved us." Psalm 46:1 reminds us that "God is our refuge and strength, a very present _____ in trouble." Ephesians 3:20 also assures us that Christ "is able to do _____ abundantly above all that we ask or think according to the _____ that worketh in us."

c. It is indispensable that we equip ourselves with the armor of God, since we are Christian soldiers. Ephesians 6:10–18 gives us a list of provisions that we need to combat against the attacks of Satan and *the rulers of the darkness of this world.* Verse 11 gives us the command: "Put on the whole _____ of God, that ye may be able to stand against the _____ (strategies) of the devil."

6. We should look for help from the pastor of a Bible-believing church.

a. It is important that we attend faithfully a Bible-believing church where they teach and practice the sound doctrine of the Bible. We must faithfully hear the preaching and teaching of God's Word in order to grow spiritually and have His direction in our life. If we do not attend church, we will be in direct disobedience to the command of God in Hebrews 10:25: "Not forsaking the _____ of ourselves together, as the manner of some is; but exhorting one another: and so much the more, as ye see the day approaching." If we are faithful in attending the Bible studies and services, we will become grounded in His Word, and God will bless us.

b. It is important that we grow in the grace of God, and intensify our walk with the Lord as we study the Word of God. Read John 15:14. Are you a friend of God? _____ We have to set time aside to read His Word, and at the same time put it into practice in obedience to Christ." The Apostle Peter commanded in 2 Peter 3:18, "But

_____ in _____, and in the knowledge of our Lord and Savior Jesus Christ."

III. What does the Bible teach about separation from worldliness?

We need to separate ourselves to those things that are honest and straightforward before God. The Apostle Paul gave the order in Romans 6:12–13, "Let not _____ therefore _____ in your mortal body, that ye should obey it in the lusts thereof. Neither yield ye your members as instruments of unrighteousness unto sin: but **yield yourselves unto God**, as those that are alive from the dead, and your members **as instruments of righteousness** unto God."

1. The Bible teaches a lot about separation from the worldly system and worldly things. It also admonishes us to be separated to God as His instruments in service to Him.

   a. God wants there to be a distinct difference between those that have given themselves to Christ and those that belong to their father, Satan. In John 17:16 Jesus Christ clearly says: "They are not of the _____, even as I am not of the _____." The spirit of the world is proud and egoistic, not humble. The spirit of this world cannot be in agreement or in harmony with the Spirit of God.

   b. The Apostle Paul exhorts the Christian against living a sensual and worldly life as mentioned in Galatians 5:16–18. Verse 16 instructs, "This I say then, walk in the Spirit, and ye shall not fulfil the lust of the _____." It is an impossibility to live in fleshly lusts and at the same time walk in conformity to the Spirit of God. We are either spiritual or worldly. How does God want you to live? _____ Paul presents in Galatians 5:19–21 a list of characteristics and practices that God hates that are of this worldly system: "Adultery, fornication, uncleanness, lasciviousness, idolatry, witchcraft, hatred, variance, emulations, wrath, strife, seditions, heresies, envyings, murders, drunkenness, revellings, and such like: of the which I tell you before, as I have also told you in time past, **that they which do such things shall _not_ inherit the _____ of God**." Are those who practice these sins condemned to eternal judgment, or are they just _worldly Christians_? _____

c. If our thoughts and desires are dedicated to temporal and earthly things, then how can we truthfully say that we love God? The Apostle John declares in 1 John 2:16, "For all that is in the world, the lust of the _____, and the lust of the _____, and the pride of _____, is not of the Father, but is of the _____." Our heart's desire should not be toward riches, honor, and carnal pleasures, such as being involved in the movie theater, television, dances, illicit sex, alcohol, drugs, the bad use of the tongue, tobacco, worldly parties and pornography. How can you love God and at the same time love and practice these worldly pleasures. 1 John 2:15 affirms, "the _____ of the Father is not in him."

d. The Christian has a different Spirit, the Holy Spirit, who lives in him. It affirms this truth in 1 Corinthians 2:12: "Now we have received, not the spirit of the _____, but the Spirit which is of _____." Paul identifies the true Christian in 2 Timothy 2:19: "Nevertheless the foundation of God standeth sure, having this seal, the Lord _____ them that are His. And, let every one that nameth the name of Christ _____ from iniquity (sin)." Matthew 6:24 says, "No man can serve _____ masters: for either he will hate the one, and love the other." The word *serve* is very important, because the will of God is that we only serve Him, and He does not want to share us with the world. (Romans 6:13) God asks for our faithfulness to Him; however, God will not impose His will on you, but asks you to be faithful in living a separated life to Him in everything. We find a very important question in Amos 3:3 regarding our separation: "Can two walk together, except they be _____?" If we truly love God, we cannot defraud Him!

e. God condemns our association with the *works of darkness*. In 2 Corinthians 6:14–17 God gives an order to those who belong to Him that must be heeded in every area of our life: "Be ye not un-equally yoked together with unbelievers: for what fellowship hath _____ with unrighteousness? and what communion hath _____ with darkness? (This *darkness* refers to the dominion of Satan.) And what concord hath Christ with Belial (another name for Satan)? or what part hath he that believeth with an _____ (one who is an unbeliever)? And what agreement hath the temple of

95

God with _____? for ye are the _____ of the living God; as God hath said, I will dwell in them, and walk in them; and I will be their God, and they shall be my people. Wherefore come out from among them, and be ye _____, saith the Lord, and touch not the unclean thing; and I will receive you, and will be a Father unto you, and ye shall be my sons and daughters, saith the Lord Almighty." We belong to God and we cannot continue our filthy living of the past. Has God changed you? _____ For what purpose? _____

f. Separation from worldly practices is one of the evidences that we love and belong to Jesus Christ. The Apostle Paul in 2 Corinthians 7:1 gives very important instructions for each child of God: "Having therefore these promises, dearly beloved, let us cleanse ourselves from all filthiness of the _____ and _____, perfecting holiness in the fear of God." Paul, writing in Romans 12:1–2, pleads with the Christians saying: "I beseech you therefore, brethren, by the mercies of God, that ye _____ your bodies a living sacrifice, holy, acceptable unto God, which is your reasonable service. And be not _____ to this world: but be ye transformed **by the renewing of your mind**, that ye may _____ what is that good, and acceptable, and perfect, will of God." Are you living according to the worldly system that wants to control your thinking and your life, or has your mind been truly transformed by Jesus Christ? _____ Is it possible for a person to be a Christian and at the same time waste his life in the search of lustful pleasures, following after the desires of this world? _____ Those who practice sin show no evidence of having been born again. They are a friend of the world and an enemy of the Lord Jesus Christ. Read carefully Matthew 7:15–20. "Wherefore by their _____ ye shall know them."

g. As true Christians, what are our obligations? It is critical that each one of us examine our associations, activities, attitudes, thoughts, what we see, what we hear and what we do in the light of the Word of God. A person of this world lives for this world. We cannot hope that he would do anything else, because that is his way of life, his person, his character and his very nature. Those who do not belong to Christ love the worldly system. They choose worldly friends, and follow the style of the world. They are in agreement with their ideas and enjoy their frivolousness, amusements, immoral activities and deplorable customs; but in the end they will be destroyed. Even the morally correct person needs the Savior. Remember what is declared in Ecclesiastes 12:14: "For God shall bring every work into _____, with every secret thing, whether it be good or whether it be evil." In no way can we live according to the desires of the flesh, and at the same time live according to the Spirit of God. James 4:4 clearly states that we cannot belong to two worlds: "Ye adulterers and adulteresses, know ye not that the friendship of the world is enmity with God? Whosoever therefore will be a _____ of the world is the _____ of God." Romans 8:6 declares, "For to be carnally minded is _____." Have your appetites changed?

_____

In contrast, the true Christian has abundant life, great opportunities to please God, and walks in true fellowship with Christ. Again Romans 8:6 continues, "but to be spiritually minded is _____ and _____." The separation of ourselves from worldly things and practices, and at the same time being busy in the things and practices that God loves is another evidence that we love God; it also shows our spiritual maturity.

2. The Bible teaches us a lot about separation from the religious traditions we practiced before we were saved.

a. Idolatry is a great sin. Read Exodus 20:4–5; Psalm 115:3–8; Psalm 135:15–18; Habakkuk 2:18–20 and Deuteronomy 7:25. God prohibits anything that takes His place, or would be used to represent Him. God requires that we be separated from all contamination of this world, both physical and spiritual as we see in 2 Corinthians 6:14–16: "Be ye not unequally yoked together with unbelievers: for what _____ hath righteousness with unrighteousness? And what communion hath light with _____? And what concord hath Christ with Belial? Or what part hath he that believeth with an infidel? And what agreement hath the temple of God with _____ (images)? For **ye** are the temple of the living God; as God hath said, I will _____ in them, and walk in them; and I will be their God, and they shall be my people." If we are God's property, how is it possible to share our being with the world or the world's religions? Those that have not abandoned things like images, relics and religious customs are acting in direct disobedience to God. If you have these things in your life, examine your heart to see if you really are of Christ. There are many that make false professions, deceiving themselves. In the letter of 3 John 1:11 the Apostle warns: "Beloved, follow not that which is evil, but that which is _____. He that doeth good is of God: but he that doeth evil hath not _____ God." This means that he is not of God! It declares that he does not know God. Anything that is more important than Jesus Christ is an idol.

b. The teachings of false teachers are extremely dangerous. God wants us to be faithful to the pure, holy, *sound doctrine* of the Word of God. 2 Timothy 4:1–4 says, "For the time will come when they will not endure _____ doctrine; but after their own _____ (carnal desires) shall they heap to themselves teachers, having itching ears." Many teach about *another Jesus, another gospel*, and speak about *another Spirit*, but they are not of God. In 2 Corinthians 11:1–4, the Apostle Paul begs the Corinthians not to have their minds *corrupted from the simplicity that is in Christ*. Colossians 2:8 warns us to, "Beware lest any man spoil you (mislead you) through philosophy and vain deceit, after the _____ of men, after the rudiments of the world, and not after Christ."

IV. Guidelines for questionable activities

There are five important principals that are helpful as "guidelines" when the Bible is not clear whether an activity is wrong for us or not. What must we do? What does the Bible say? **When there is doubt, ask the following questions:**

1. Is this activity really necessary? Hebrews 12:1 says, "Wherefore seeing we also are compassed about with so great a cloud of witnesses, let us lay aside every _____, and the sin which doth so easily beset us, and let us run with patience the race that is set before us." Are the things or the activities in which I am participating a "weight" on my life so that I cannot serve the Lord Jesus Christ as I should?

2. Is this activity helpful for my spiritual life or the spiritual life of others? The Apostle Paul says in 1 Corinthians 6:12, "All things are lawful

(speaking of things that are correct and good) unto me, but all things are not _____ (fitting)." Does my thought-life affect my desires and my actions? _____ Please write the meaning of Romans 14:7: "For none of us liveth to himself, and no man dieth to himself." _____

_____

If your thought-life is evil, your actions will become evil. Why?

_____

_____

3. Is this activity, person or thing having a negative influence on me? Is it a habit that is dominating my life? In the second part of 1 Corinthians 6:12, the Apostle Paul talks about good things that cannot be classified as bad: "all things are lawful for me, but I will not be brought under the _____ of any." Am I being led and controlled by the Holy Spirit, or by other people or activities?

4. What would Christ do? 1 John 2:6 simply says, "He that _____ he abideth in him ought himself also so to walk, even as he walked." How am I walking? Is my walk or manner of life in harmony with Jesus Christ? Is my daily living in obedience to the Word of God and pleasing to the Lord? Am I following carefully in His steps?

5. By being involved in this activity or possessing this thing, am I giving a good testimony of Christ Jesus to those who see me? The Apostle Paul in 1 Thessalonians 5:22 gives a solid command telling us to: "Abstain from all _____ of evil." Colossians 3:17 says, "And whatsoever ye do in word or deed, do _____ in the name of the Lord Jesus, giving thanks to God and the Father by him." Am I glorifying God with what I do?

Summary:

The Christian has daily battles with sin in his life. These conflicts come from the WORLD, the FLESH and the DEVIL. We have all the resources from God to enable us to have victory in our life. These resources are: (1) Trust in God; (2) Be strengthened in His Word; (3) Watch and pray; (4) Recognize and confess our sins; (5) Recognize our weaknesses and the power of God; (6) Look for the help from a Bible-believing church and pastor. God has promised to provide us with a way out of temptations. We must be submissive to God and resist the devil. We must put on the whole armor of God. We must confess our sins to God and receive His forgiveness. We need to give our full attention to being God's instruments of righteousness, separated from the world and its worldly practices.

REVIEW QUESTIONS
CHAPTER 7 — POWER TO OVERCOME TEMPTATIONS AND TRIALS

1. What is the only guide for all doctrine and practice in the life of the believer?

    _____

2. 1 John 1:8, was written for believers. Who of us are incapable of sinning? (some religious leaders), (few), (no one). Please underline the correct answer.

3. Do Christians have spiritual conflicts?_____ Why? _____

    _____

4. What are some characteristics of a life controlled by the new nature of the believer? (Galatians 5:22–23) _____

    _____

5. Name the three principal enemies of all Christians.

    1. _____

    2. _____

    3. _____

6. God helps us to triumph over all temptations from the world, the flesh, and the devil. (1 Corinthians 10:13) "God is _____, who will not _____ (permit) you to be tempted above that ye are able; but will with the temptation also make a way to _____, that ye may be able to _____ it."

7. God has given us two means of having communion with Him. It is through the _____ and _____.

8. How does the battle for the Christian differ from the battles which are fought between two nations? _____

_____

9. Why should a Christian be separated from worldliness? _____

_____

_____

10. Why does a true Christian have to separate himself from his past religious practices?_____

_____

11. Which Spirit now dwells in the life of the true Christian? _____

12. Name five guidelines for the Christian regarding questionable activities.

    a. _____

    b. _____

    c. _____

    d. _____

    e. _____

13. How can a Christian have victory over the three principal enemies? _____

_____

_____

_____

Please memorize 1 Corinthians 10:13 and write it in your own words. _____

_____

_____

_____

_____

Please send your answers to the questions and any doubts that you might have regarding this lesson to the Bible Institute Correspondence Department: philippi@becoming-a-christian.org

How can we grow strong spiritually? We need the intake of God's Word daily in order to have good spiritual health. Notice how this is emphasized in the next chapter.

— Chapter Eight —

The Importance of Bible Study

All Scripture is given by inspiration of God, and is profitable for doctrine,
for reproof, for correction, for instruction in righteousness:
That the man of God may be perfect, thoroughly furnished unto all good works.
2 Timothy 3:16–17

Why must we study the Word of God?

Many Christians know very little about what the Bible says and teaches. Some of those that read the Bible limit their knowledge, reading only the portions of the New and Old Testament that please them, or study certain subjects which are important to them. Studying the Bible in this way brings us to incomplete and uncertain conclusions. Moreover, it is a proud and wrong attitude to believe that we are able to choose the important parts to read and ignore the rest of the Bible. One must study the **whole Bible.**

Certain people say that they have read the Bible, but they do not understand it. Also, many have doubts and believe that the Bible contains fables or errors. It is our desire to help you to understand and appreciate the Bible. The Bible is a letter given by the Spirit of God to men. God speaks to us by means of the Bible, showing us His love and His will for all mankind. It teaches us all that God wants us to know about Himself, and His plan for our life. The Apostle Paul reminds us in 1 Thessalonians 2:13: "For this cause also thank we God without ceasing, because, when ye received the Word of ___ ___ which ye heard of us, ye received it not as the word of men, but as it is in truth, the Word of _____, which effectually _____ also in you that believe." The Bible gives us the reason for our existence and it teaches us the reason for our life. It is the only authority over our lives and we must be in submission to it in all doctrine and practice. God wants His Word to dwell abundantly in us.

I. The divine inspiration of the Bible

1. God is the Author of the Bible.
   The Author of the Bible is God, the Holy Spirit. He directed those that wrote each book and lead them in a way that the words used are the ones that God wanted them to write. The only true and living God used and directed more than forty men, from shepherds to kings, with different abilities and education, living in distinct ages and places, during a period of 1,500 years, so that the Bible could be complete. However, there is unity and harmony in all of its parts. The Holy Scriptures were finalized toward the end of the first century when the Apostle John finished the book of Revelation. Since then, many have tried to give importance to dreams, visions, or other messages from men; but the Bible is the <u>only</u> inspired voice of God given to man. 2 Timothy 3: 16 teaches: "All Scripture is given by _____ of God, and is _____ for doctrine, for reproof, for correction, for instruction in righteousness." The Apostle Peter in 2 Peter 1:20–21 confirms the same truth: "Knowing this first, that no prophecy of the scripture is of any _____ interpretation. For the prophecy came not in old time by the _____ of man: but holy men of God spake as they were _____ by the Holy Ghost." It is confirmed in Hebrews 1:1–2 that "God, ... hath in these last days spoken unto us by his _____."

2. God gives power by means of the Bible.
   God fortifies and encourages us through His Word. Ephesians 6:10 says, "Finally, my brethren, be _____ in the Lord, and in the power of His _____." Ephesians 3:20–21 also says, "Now unto him that is _____ to do exceeding abundantly above all that we ask or think, according to the _____ that _____ in us, unto _____ be glory in the church by Christ Jesus throughout all ages, world without end." The Word of God produces changes in our life! Read 1 Thessalonians 1:5.

3. All the Bible is true.
   Jesus Christ said in John 18:37: "To this end was I born, and for this cause came I into the world, that I should **bear witness** unto the _____.

Every one that is of the truth heareth my voice." Jesus gave testimony that the Bible is true. Because of this He also said in John 8:47: "He that is of God heareth God's _____." Psalm 119:160 declares: "Thy word is _____ from the beginning: and every one of thy righteous judgments endureth for ever." Jesus Christ prayed in John 17:17, "Sanctify them through thy _____: thy word is _____."

II. The content of the Bible

The Bible, being verbally inspired by God, is perfect and without error in its content. It is a library of 66 books, which is divided into two parts called, Old and New Testaments, and each book is divided into chapters, and each chapter into verses. **These divisions are not inspired by God,** but have been added to help locate passages much easier. The major part of the Old Testament was written in Hebrew. The major part of the New Testament was written in Greek. The Bible contains the physical and spiritual history of man from the beginning of time. It speaks in general and in a specific form about the chosen nation of Israel, and God's treatment of them. In the Bible, God's Divine plan is revealed for all mankind. In the Bible are found all of the doctrines that establish the faith and the practice of the church of Jesus Christ. The principal person of the Bible is the Lord Jesus Christ, the only God and Savior of the world. The Word of God is our spiritual food, our guide, and our protection from sin; it stimulates our spiritual growth. The Old Testament looks forward, and the New Testament looks back to Jesus Christ.

Old Testament ☞ **Jesus Christ** ☜ New Testament

1. What are the six <u>names</u> that God uses when He refers to His Word in Psalm 19?

   (1) 19:7 _____

   (2) 19:7 _____ _____

   (3) 19:8 _____

   (4) 19:8 _____

   (5) 19:9 _____

   (6) 19:9 _____

2. What are the six <u>characteristics</u> of God's Word referred to in Psalm 19? (In other words, what is it like?)

(1) 19:7 _____

(2) 19:7 _____

(3) 19:8 _____

(4) 19:8 _____

(5) 19:9 _____

(6) 19:9 _____

3. How does the Word of God benefit us?

(1) 19:7 _____

(2) 19:7 _____

(3) 19:8 _____

(4) 19:8 _____

(5) 19:9 _____

III. The divisions of the Bible

1. THE OLD TESTAMENT contains 39 books, all written before Christ was born.

   a. The Law or the Pentateuch (5 books)

   b. The History of Israel (12 books)

   c. The Poems (5 books)

   d. The Prophets (17 books)

2. THE NEW TESTAMENT contains 27 books

   a. The History of Christ (the 4 Gospels)

   b. The History of the Primitive Church (1 book)

   c. The Doctrine (21 epistles to the Christians and to the churches)

   d. Prophecy – Revelation (1 book) (Besides this book, there are many prophecies throughout the Bible.)

Homework: Please memorize the names of the 27 books of the New Testament in their correct order. Later, learn the names of the 39 books of the Old Testament in their correct order. In this way you will know how to locate the different books of the Bible, find the passages, and follow along during the teaching of the Word of God and in the worship services of the church.

IV. How can we receive the greatest benefit from the message of God?

1. We need to hear the Word of God.

   We can hear the Word of God in different manners: by attending church services, attending Bible studies, listening to good Christian programs on the radio (if they are of sound doctrine), and hearing audio tapes of the Word of God. The Apostle Paul tells us in Romans 10:17 how the *faith of God* comes to us: "So then _____ cometh by hearing, and hearing by the _____ of _____." Why is it important to listen to the preaching of the Word of God? _____

2. We need to read the Word of God.

   Our personal reading of the Bible has the power to transform our lives. An effective method is to have a daily plan for reading the Word of God, and have communion with God through prayer. Possibly the best way would be to read three chapters from some book of the Bible each day. We suggest that you start with the Gospels of Mark and John, after this the letter to the Romans, and then continue with a plan to finish reading the entire Bible. Hebrews 4:12 expresses very well what the Word of God does in our life: "For the Word of God is quick, and powerful, and sharper than any two–edged _____, piercing even to the dividing asunder of soul and spirit, and of the joints and marrow, and is a _____ of the thoughts and intents of the heart."

3. We need to study the Word of God.

   The Word of God is the only guide and true authority in which we can fully trust. The order given in 2 Timothy 2:15 is important: "Study to shew thyself approved unto God, a _____ that needeth not to be ashamed, rightly _____ (interpreting) the word of _____."
   In order to be grounded in the Word of God, it is important to attend the Bible studies and worship services of your church. 1 Peter 2:2 tells us, "As newborn babes, _____ the sincere milk of the Word, that ye

may _____ thereby." We recommend the use of other books and commentaries for additional study. The pastor of your church can recommend some Bible study books and courses so that you can continue studying at home. If you do not have a pastor, you can write to us for information.

In 2 Timothy 3:16–17, several ways are mentioned as to how God uses His Word in our lives. It is:

- Profitable for _____ (teaching)

- Profitable for _____ (investigation)

- Profitable for _____ (discipline)

- Profitable for _____ in righteousness:

- Profitable for _____ (maturing)

For what purpose does God do all this work in and for us? 2 Timothy 3:17 declares, "That the man of God may be _____ (mature), thoroughly furnished unto all good _____." God wants to prepare us day by day so that we can be better persons and serve Him better.

4. We need to meditate on the Word of God.

As our daily food is important for our body, so is the Word of God for our soul and spirit. Joshua 1:8 helps us to appreciate the importance of meditation in the Bible for our edification: "This book of the law shall not depart out of thy mouth; but thou shalt **meditate** therein _____ and _____, that thou mayest _____ to do according to _____ that is written therein: for then thou shalt make thy way prosperous, and then thou shalt have _____ success." When reading a portion of God's Word, take time to meditate on it and think about how to apply it in your life. Afterwards, put into practice what you have learned. We read in Ezra 7:10, "For Ezra had prepared his heart to _____ the law of the Lord, and to _____ it, and to _____ in Israel statutes and judgments." Isaiah 26:3 declares, "Thou wilt keep him in perfect peace, whose _____ is stayed on thee: because he trusteth in thee." Also, Psalm 1:2 shows the desires of the heart of the believer: "But his delight is in the law of the Lord; and in his law doth he _____ day and night."

5. We need to memorize the Word of God.

    Memorizing the Word of God enriches our lives, and we also receive great blessing from God. By memorizing Bible verses, we are spiritually strengthened and our thoughts are steadfast in His Word to help us in times of testing. King David declared in Psalm 119:11: "Thy Word have I _____ in mine heart, that I might not _____ against thee." Only through memorizing God's Word can we maintain the stability in our lives that God desires. A good practice is to memorize at least one Scripture verse each week. This will have a significant impact on your life and will help you to grow spiritually.

    When we memorize Scripture we are making preparations to use it in the future. The Apostle Peter taught in 1 Peter 3:15, "Be ready always to give an _____ to every man that asketh you a reason of the hope that is in you with meekness and fear." Memorizing the Word of God is the best way to be prepared to testify to others. The Word of God should become part of our very being as is ordered in Colossians 3:16: "Let the word of Christ _____ in you _____ in all wisdom; teaching and admonishing one another."

6. We need to obey the Word of God.

    It is indispensable that we put into practice the teaching that we receive from the Bible. In Romans 16:19 the Apostle Paul expressed his gratitude saying: "For your obedience is come abroad unto all men. I am glad therefore on your behalf: but yet I would have you _____ unto that which is good, and _____ concerning evil." In Luke 11:28 Jesus Christ declared: "Yea rather, (more) blessed are they that _____ the word of God, and _____ it (obey it)." We must obey 1 Peter 1:14, "As _____ children, not fashioning yourselves according to the former lusts in your ignorance." At times our friends, circumstances, or employers ask us to do things that are incorrect, violating Biblical principals. Our response to them should always be the same that the apostles of Jesus gave in Acts 5:27–29: "We ought to _____ **God** rather than men." You are now a new person in Christ and your life needs to be governed by Him and His Word.

7. We need to teach the Word of God to others.

    We need to prepare ourselves through the study of God's Word so that we can teach others correctly. The Apostle Paul reminds us in

2 Timothy 2:2, "The things that thou hast heard of me among many witnesses, the same commit thou to _____ men, who shall be able to _____ others also." In Matthew 4:19 we see Jesus appointing His apostles: "Follow me, and I will make you _____ of men." After Christ Jesus had taught His apostles, He sent them two by two to proclaim the Gospel. They were well equipped with His teachings. Jesus gave them, and also gave us the great commission in Mark 16:15: "Go ye into _____ the world, and _____ the _____ to every creature." In Matthew 28:19–20 Jesus Christ commands His disciples saying, "_____ ye therefore, and _____ all nations, baptizing them in the name of the Father, and of the Son, and of the Holy Spirit." This command of Christ applies to us also. We have to share His glorious message with the world around us. Psalm 126:5–6 encourages us saying: "They that _____ in tears shall reap in joy. He that goeth forth and weepeth, _____ precious seed, shall doubtless come again with _____, bringing his sheaves with him."

Summary:

The Bible, inspired by the Holy Spirit of God, is composed of 66 books, which are divided into the Old and the New Testaments. The principal focus of the Bible is on the Lord Jesus Christ, the only God and Savior of the world. The Bible presents from the beginning the physical and spiritual history of sinful man. The Bible is spiritual food, a guide, and a protection from sin; it stimulates our spiritual growth. To be beneficial to us, we have to hear the Word of God, read it, study it, memorize it, and meditate upon it. By doing all this, the final results should be our obedience with all our heart to the teachings of God's Word. Through the Word of God, the Holy Spirit teaches us doctrine and practical Christian living. We cannot permit other authorities to guide us. God's Word teaches us that we cannot give our attention to visions, dreams or other spectacular manifestations, but only to His Word. Those things are not of God.

REVIEW QUESTIONS

CHAPTER 8 — THE IMPORTANCE OF BIBLE STUDY

1. Who is the only true Author of the Bible? The _____ _____

2. How many men did God use to write the Bible? _____

3. The major divisions of the Old Testament are:

    • The _____ or The _____ ___

    • The _____ of Israel

    • The _____ ____

    • The _____

4. The major divisions of the New Testament are:

    • The history of _____ (4 Gospels)

    • The history of _____

    • The _____ (21 letters)

    • The _____ or _____ ___ (1 book)

5. In 2 Timothy 3:16–17, what four ways does God use His Word in our life?

    (1) It is profitable for _____ _____ (teaching)

    (2) It is profitable for _____ (investigation)

    (3) It is profitable for _____ _____ (discipline)

    (4) It is profitable for _____ _____ in righteousness:

    (5) It is profitable for _____ (maturing)

6. What must we do to take advantage of God's teaching?

    (1) _____ Word of God

    (2) _____ Word of God

    (3) _____ Word of God

    (4) _____ Word of God

    (5) _____ Word of God

(6) _____ Word of God

(7) _____ Word of God

You can read the Bible in 80 hours, but I suggest that you try to read at least one to three chapters each day. If you read three chapters each day and five on Sunday you will be able to read the Bible through in one year. I encourage you to memorize the ten key verses at the beginning of each lesson. It is important that you also learn other Bible verses given in these lessons.

————————◆◆✕◆◆————————

Please send your answers to the questions and any doubts that you might have regarding this lesson to the Bible Institute Correspondence Department: philippi@becoming-a-christian.org

— Chapter Nine —

The Importance of Prayer

For we have not an high priest which cannot be touched with the feeling of our infirmities; but was in all points tempted like as we are, yet without sin. Let us therefore come boldly unto the throne of grace, that we may obtain mercy, and find grace to help in time of need. Hebrews 4:15–16

God desires to have communion with us.

Prayer is intimate communion with God. With confidence and a contrite and humble heart, we should take time to be alone with Him. Prayer is an expression of the most intimate thoughts of our heart to God. It is a privilege to be able to speak directly with God the Father through Jesus Christ. If we love Him, we will want to spend time daily with Him. God has shown His love to us, so we should respond to that love. The best form of expressing real love is by seeking opportunities to be with the one we love.

I. Why should we pray?

1. We pray because it is a privilege, and at the same time it is our solemn responsibility.

   Our key verse for this lesson gives us an invitation to come boldly before God. What a privilege! Prayer is necessary in order to receive His mercy, grace, and help. In the Old Testament, God said in 2 Chronicles 7:14: "If _____ people, which are called by _____ name, shall _____ themselves, and _____ ___, and seek my face, and turn from their wicked ways; then will I _____ from heaven, and will

_____ their sin, and will heal their land." In Ephesians 6:18–19 Paul insisted that we be, "Praying always with all prayer and supplication in the Spirit, and watching thereunto with _____ perseverance and supplication for all saints; and for me, that utterance may be given unto me, that I may open my mouth boldly, to make _____ the mystery of the Gospel."

2. We pray because it is an example given by Christ, the apostles, and the early church.

Jesus Christ made it a practice to talk to His heavenly Father, as revealed in Mark 1:35: "And in the morning, rising up a great while before day, he went out, and departed into a solitary place, and there _____." Luke 6:12 shows the importance that He gave to a special time of prayer: "And it came to pass in those days, that he went out into a mountain to _____, and continued all _____ in prayer to God." How much more do we need to spend time in prayer!

Great importance was given to prayer by the early church. They did not permit outside distractions to crowd in and prevent prayer. In Acts 6:2, the apostles said, "It is not reason that we should leave the _____ of God, and serve tables." The correct solution to a need was presented in Acts 6:3–4: "Wherefore, brethren, look (search) ye out among you seven men of honest report, full of the Holy Spirit and _____, whom we may appoint over this business. But we will give ourselves continually to _____, and to the _____ of the Word."

3. Praying will keep us from falling into temptation.

God knows that we will always have battles with sin; for this reason He made the provision to have those sins forgiven and receive daily cleansing. The tendency to forget the need to pray opens the door to temptation, which can result in sin. Many times the activities of the day and the urgencies of work distract our attention from this important communion with God. In Matthew 26:41 Jesus said to the apostles: "Watch and pray, that ye enter not into _____: the spirit indeed is willing, but the flesh is weak." Because we are His children we should not neglect His fellowship. The remedy is to plan a time and place to have this fellowship everyday.

II. Who can pray?

1. The repentant sinner can pray. God heard the publican pray, and the thief on the cross who was next to Jesus as he pleaded for mercy. God also wants to hear your prayers. David prayed to God in Psalm 51:17, "The sacrifices of God are the broken spirit: a _____ and _____ heart, O God, thou wilt not despise." When God hears our repentant and humble prayers, He shows mercy. The convincing story of Cornelius, described in Acts 10:1–48, shows how he prayed to God with all sincerity and God heard him.

2. His children can pray, and God wants to have communion with them. The Word of God says in 1 Peter 3:12, "For the _____ of the Lord are over the righteous, and His _____ are open unto their prayers: but the _____ of the Lord is _____ them that do evil." Some say, *prayer is an avenue where all can travel.* Is this true?_____

3. Those who fulfill the conditions, put forth by God, can pray! God gives us His conditions for our prayers to be answered. God requires holiness in our lives. He desires that our lives be clean. God wants to give His forgiveness and cleanse us. He assures us in 1 John 1:9 saying, "If we confess our _____, he is faithful and just to forgive us our sin, and to _____ us from all unrighteousness." Paul instructs all believers to clean up their lives from all the contaminations of the flesh and the mind. This includes the influences that can cause us to drift from that holy life which honors and glorifies the Lord Jesus. Besides this, He wants us to cleanse our life from the things that affect our spirit, and damage our relationship and harmony with God. Paul exhorts us, in 2 Corinthians 7:1, to clean up our lives: "Having therefore these promises, dearly beloved, let us _____ ourselves from all filthiness of the flesh and spirit, perfecting _____ in the fear of God." This passage reminds us of the command given by God in 2 Chronicles 7:11–15.

III. Where should we pray?

Should we only pray in a church at some altar? No! God desires that we pray to Him wherever we are and at any time. The apostles prayed everywhere and in all circumstances, and we should certainly have the same practice. 1 Timothy 2:8 says, "I will therefore that men pray _____."

We should pray everywhere. We can be in an attitude of fellowship with God and talk with Him in prayer, no matter what the circumstances are that surround us. **Many interpret wrongly the last part of 1 Timothy 2:8.** It says, "<u>lifting up holy hands, without wrath and doubting</u>." **This has nothing to do with our physical hands**, but only has reference in a symbolic manner to help us realize that God sees the **sin** that we have committed. God insists that we recognize the sin in our life, repent, and that we confess it to Him. This is the only way that God can see our *holy hands (our holy life)* as we daily practice holiness in our life. All unconfessed sin affects our life, and it affects others. A bad testimony can also cause someone else to turn away from the Lord.

IV. When can we pray?

1 Thessalonians 5:17 says, "Pray without ceasing." We should always be in an attitude conducive to prayer, in any place, and with the confidence that He is present and hears us. We should be always in intimate communion with God whenever or wherever we may be, regardless of what we may be doing. We should pray in moments of need and joy. King David expressed himself in Psalm 55:17 in this way: "_____ and _____, and at _____, I will pray and cry aloud: and He shall hear my voice." Praying should be as natural as breathing. Ephesians 6:18 says, "Praying _____ with all prayer and supplication in the Spirit, and watching thereunto with all perseverance and supplication for all _____ (has reference to those who belong to God)."

V. How should we pray?

1. We should go to God with reverence and adoration. We should give Him all honor and praise, not only with our mind and mouth, but also with our life. God is Sovereign, Omnipotent, Omniscient, Omnipresent, Eternal, King of Kings, and Lord of Lords. The Apostle Paul let words of adoration flow from his lips in 1 Timothy 6:15–16, saying: "Which in his times he shall shew, who is the blessed and only Potentate, the King of kings, and Lord of Lords; Who only hath immortality, dwelling in the light which no man can approach unto; whom no man hath seen, nor can see: to whom be _____ and power everlasting. Amen." Many of the Psalms are prayers of praise and adoration to God. An example is Psalm 104:1, "Bless the Lord, O my soul, O Lord my God, thou art

very great; thou art clothed with _____ and majesty." (Other good examples of praise are Psalm 29:2; Psalm 34:3; Isaiah 25:1.)

Many make the mistake of referring to God with such refrains as *the man upstairs*, etc. Never should we use such expressions in reference to God, for it is a great lack of respect! Listen to the advice given in Ecclesiastes 5:2: "Be not _____ with thy mouth, and let not thine heart be _____ to utter anything before God: for God is in _____, and thou upon _____: therefore let thy words be _____." It is important to speak with all respect and reverence when we mention the name, God. Our prayers should not be frivolous, self-centered or irresponsible. It is wrong to speak with absurdities, and not think about what we say.

2. We should approach God with the intention of receiving cleansing for our sin. Paul encourages us in Hebrew 10:21–22 saying: "And having an high priest over the house of God; let us draw near with a _____ heart in full assurance of _____, having our hearts sprinkled from an evil _____, and our bodies washed with pure _____ (the Word of God)." Here it speaks symbolically to help us realize that God sees our life. It is necessary to confess our sins to Christ and to ask for forgiveness, so that God will hear us. Psalm 66:18 warns, "If I regard iniquity (sin) in my heart, the Lord will not _____ me." The confession of sin in prayer each day is necessary to maintain our communion and a good relationship with God. What promise does God make when we confess our sins to Him, and separate ourselves to Him for His use? Proverbs 28:13 declares, "He that covereth his sins shall not _____: but whoso _____ and _____ them shall have mercy." Jesus Christ requires that we confess our sins to receive His pardon and cleansing. Unconfessed sin has many bad effects on our physical and spiritual life. It is also a bad testimony to the unsaved around us and gives them reason to reject the message of the Gospel.

3. It is important for us to express our gratitude to God for everything that He has done in our life, and for all the provisions of each day that He gives us: our food, our clothes, our home, the measure of health that we have, our work, our family members, our protection, our clothes, our changed life in Christ, the Word of God, and spiritual teaching. The Apostle Paul admonishes us in Colossians 4:2 to, "Continue in

_____, and watch in the same with _____." In 1 Corinthians 15:57, he gives thanks to God for victories in his life: "But thanks be to God, which giveth us the _____ through our Lord Jesus Christ." Also in Ephesians 5:20 the Apostle Paul gives another instruction regarding our gratitude: "Giving _____ always for _____ things unto God and the Father, in the name of our Lord Jesus Christ." Colossians 3:17 reminds us to express gratitude for all that we do: "And whatsoever ye do in word or deed, do all in the name of the Lord Jesus, giving thanks to God and the Father by him." Prayer should be an act of gratitude. God teaches us that we should always be thankful for all that we receive. Upon praying, we should express this gratitude to the Lord. It is a holy privilege to be able to go to God, enjoy fellowship together and talk to Him about our joys and our sorrows. The expressions of King David in the Psalms many times are expressions of the deeper feelings of his heart. Psalm 31:19 exclaims, "Oh how great is Thy goodness, which thou hast laid up for them that fear thee; which thou hast wrought for them that trust in thee before the sons of men!" When we think of God's kindness, of His grace, of His love and of His mercy, how can we help but express our gratitude to Him!

4. God puts obedience as a condition for our prayers to be answered. We must obey the Word of God. 1 John 3:22 says, "Whatsoever we ask, we receive of Him, because we keep His _____ (His instructions), and do those things that are pleasing in His sight." In the Gospel of John 15:7 Jesus states, "If ye _____ in me, and my words _____ in you, ye shall ask what you will, and it shall be done unto you." God wants us to be obedient to His Word in order to receive the answers to our prayers.

5. God commands us to pray according to His will, not according to what we desire. The Apostle John, in 1 John 5:14–15, teaches us a very important truth: "This is the confidence that we have in Him, that, if we ask any thing according to His will, He _____ us: And if we know that He _____ us, whatsoever we ask, we know that we have the petitions that we desired of Him." It is important for us to pray according to the teaching of God's Word. In this way we know our requests will be in agreement with God and not just according to what we think that we need. When He does not give us what we request, we should recognize that He knows what is best for us. We need to ask God

for wisdom so that we can please Him, even in our requests. James 1:5 says, "If any of you lack _____, let him ask of God, that giveth to all men liberally, and upbraideth not; and it shall be _____ him." The more we read God's Word, the more we can understand the will of God.

Prayer is not a mystical exercise that Christians use to twist the arm of God in order to obligate Him to concede to their petitions. We should not pass the time fasting to obligate God to give us what we want. We cannot negotiate with God in order to receive our petition. It is indispensable for us to have the same attitude of Christ Jesus as expressed in Luke 22:42: "not my _____, but thine, be done." The answer to the prayer of the Apostle Paul in 2 Corinthians 12:8–9 was "No." God answered him by saying, "My grace is _____ for thee: for my strength is made perfect in weakness." Sometimes we receive a negative answer because we have asked for the wrong things. James 4:3 confirms this fact, "Ye ask, and receive not, because ye ask _____, that ye may consume it upon your lusts." Even though God knows beforehand what we need, He still wants to hear from us. God always answers our prayers. Sometimes He says, *Yes*. Sometimes He says, *No*. On other occasions God tells us, *Wait*. Always remember that **God is Sovereign**.

6. The Holy Spirit continually helps us in prayer in a way that it is difficult for us to understand. Many times we do not know what we should request, or how to request it. The Holy Spirit is continually helping us to pray. Romans 8:26 says, "Likewise the Spirit also helpeth our infirmities (weaknesses): for we _____ not what we should pray for as we ought: but the Spirit itself maketh _____ for us with groanings which cannot be uttered." This passage indicates that sometimes our petitions cannot be expressed easily. The Holy Spirit, knowing our heart and our needs, intercedes for us. He will communicate our petition to the Father as it should be; and besides this, the Spirit of God makes requests for us according to the perfect will of God. It states this in Romans 8:27, "And He that searcheth the hearts knoweth what is the mind of the Spirit, because He maketh _____ for the saints according to the _____ of God." What a comfort!

7. We should pray to God the Father in the name of Jesus Christ. Jesus declared in John 15:16: "Ye have not chosen me, but I have chosen you, and ordained you, that ye should go and bring forth _____, and

that your _____ should remain: that whatsoever ye shall ask of the Father in my _____, He may give it you." We are always in the presence of God; therefore we lift our hearts to the *throne of grace* through Jesus Christ our Lord. The Bible teaches us that we should never pray to a *saint*, to the virgin Mary or any other person. The Bible is clear when it states in 1 Timothy 2:5 that "there is one God, and one _____ between God and men, the man Christ Jesus." He is God and man at the same time. Having ascended physically into heaven, He intercedes before God the Father on our behalf.

8. We should pray with faith. James 1:6 says, "But let him ask in faith, nothing wavering. For he that _____ is like a wave of the sea driven with the wind and tossed." Instead of worrying, being concerned, or frustrated because of our problems and needs, what should we do? The Apostle Paul tells us in Philippians 4:6, "But in everything by _____ and supplication with thanksgiving let your _____ be made known unto God."

9. We must pray with sincerity. Hebrews 10:21–22 encourages us saying; "And having an high priest (Jesus Christ) over the house of God; Let us draw near with a _____ (sincere) heart in full assurance of faith, having our hearts sprinkled from an evil conscience, and our bodies washed with pure water." Reading Jeremiah 29:12–13, we see why the Lord heard their prayers, "Then shall ye call upon me, and ye shall go and pray unto me, and I will hearken unto you. And ye shall seek me, and find me, when ye shall search for me with _____ your _____."

10. Should we utilize prayers that are memorized? God does not permit repetitions of prayers. Matthew 6:7–8 teaches us that we should not use memorized prayers or useless repetition in prayer: "But when ye pray, use not vain _____, as the heathen do: for they think that they shall be heard for their _____ speaking. Be not ye therefore like unto them."

11. We should not neglect this responsibility of prayer. It is our responsibility to be alert, and to maintain the communication lines open with the Lord, by praying for daily help; for we recognize the seriousness of this life and the fact of the soon return of our Lord and Savior Jesus Christ to earth for us. For this reason Hebrews 10:25 advises us: "Not

forsaking the _____ of ourselves together, as the manner of some is; but exhorting one another: and so much the more, as ye see the day approaching." We need to meet together as the *body of Christ* to worship, hear the preaching of God's Word and to pray. In Mark 14:38 the Lord told us to, "Watch and _____." The expression *watch* means – *be alert*. It is a necessity for us to be alert to the dangers that try to derail us from the privileged path of intimate fellowship with God. We have to be serious with ourselves and maintain our prayer time with Him.

12. We need to maintain order when we pray in a group. It is a joy to be united in prayer with others, but this does not mean that there should be more than one person praying at the same time. While another prays we should be quiet and attentive to the petitions of the one praying so that we can be scriptural and say *Amen*. The word *amen* means – *May it be so*. This shows we are in agreement regarding the request being made. This teaching is found in 1 Corinthians 14:16: "Else when thou shalt bless with the spirit, how shall he that occupieth the room of the unlearned say _____ at thy giving of thanks, seeing he understandeth not what thou sayest?" God is not the author of confusion nor does he permit it. The Apostle Paul insists in 1 Corinthians 14:40: "Let all things be done decently and in _____." We must be vigilant to not allow the error of emotionalism to creep into our lives and the church through those who desire to make prayer a great emotion of ecstasy. Disorder is in direct disobedience to God's Word. Psalm 37:4 says, "Delight thyself also in the Lord: and he shall give thee the desires of thine _____." Are you obeying and honoring God in the way you pray and live? God wants us to have order in our homes, in our places of work, and in the church.

VI. For whom should we pray?

The Bible teaches a great deal regarding the persons for whom we should pray. Through prayer we can help many people. The Bible, in both the Old and New Testaments, gives many examples of God's servants who prayed. We should intercede for physical, emotional, material, and most of all, spiritual needs." The love and concern of the Apostle Paul is clearly seen in 1 Thessalonians 3:10: "Night and day _____ exceedingly that we might see your face, and might perfect (bring about maturity) that which is _____ in your faith?"

1. We need to pray for ourselves. Jeremiah 33:3 instructs us to: "_____ unto me, and I will _____ thee, and _____ thee great and mighty things, which thou knowest not." God continually blesses our lives as we continue to call upon Him. As we continue to pray for our own selves, remember the testimony of the Psalmist in Psalm 73:28: "But it is _____ for me to draw near to God: I have put my trust in the Lord God, that I may _____ all thy works." We need to express our love as we show gratitude to the Lord for what He has done for us. He enriches our life far beyond our comprehension!

2. We must pray for our family and friends, for believers and for unbelievers. Jesus Christ prayed for unbelievers and even his enemies who would someday place their trust in Him, repent of their sin and give themselves to Him. Jesus Christ prayed in John 17:20: "Neither pray I for these alone, but for _____ also which shall _____ on me through their _____." A person can only come to the Lord for salvation by the power and grace of God. We should pray that God would work in the hearts of our friends and family who do not know the Lord as their Savior. Do you pray with concern for others?

3. It is important that we pray for the brethren in the faith. Every true Christian forms part of a great family, the family of God. We need to pray one for another. In Ephesians 6:18 the Apostle Paul reminds us: "Praying always with all prayer and supplication in the Spirit, and watching thereunto with all perseverance and supplication for all _____." (The *saints* are all the brethren in the faith.) The Apostle Paul expresses the great need of praying for others in Colossians 1:9–10: "For this cause we also, since the day we heard it, do not _____ to pray for you, and to desire that ye might be filled with the knowledge of His will in all _____ and _____ understanding. That ye might walk worthy of the Lord unto all pleasing, being fruitful in every good work, and increasing in the knowledge of God." In Ephesians 1:15–23, the Apostle Paul prayed for the spiritual progress of the brethren. Our petitions are important to God, therefore we should pray not only for ourselves, but also for the spiritual needs of others.

4. The Apostle Paul prayed for the sick. In Philippians 2:27, Paul prayed for Epaphroditus: "For indeed he was _____ nigh unto death: but God had mercy on him; and not on him only, but on _____ also, lest

I should have sorrow upon sorrow." James 5:14–16 asks the question: "Is any sick among you? Let him call for the elders of the church; and let them pray over him, anointing him with oil in the name of the Lord: And the prayer of faith shall _____ (heal) the sick, and the Lord shall raise him up; and if he have committed sins, they shall be _____ him. Confess your faults one to another, and pray one for another, that ye may be healed. The effectual fervent prayer of a _____ man availeth much."

5. It is important to pray for God's servants who are active in the ministry. These servants of the Lord are those who work in the ministry to win souls for Christ and help others to grow in their spiritual life. They are pastors, teachers, missionaries, evangelists and other workers. The Apostle Paul made the request in 2 Thessalonians 3:1–2: "Finally, brethren, _____ for us, that the word of the Lord may have free course, and be _____, even as it is with you: And that we may be delivered from unreasonable and wicked men: for all men have not faith." We can help these ministers of God by praying for their spiritual life, for their ministry, and for their personal needs. The Apostle Paul, in Ephesians 6:19–20, requested them to pray, "for me, that utterance may be given unto me, that I may _____ my mouth boldly, to make known the mystery of the _____, for which I am an ambassador in bonds: that therein I may speak boldly, as I ought to speak." We should all pray for each other, that we might speak with boldness to our lost family and friends.

6. We should pray for the government authorities. The Apostle Paul commanded in 1 Timothy 2:1–2: "I exhort therefore, that, first of all, supplications, prayers, intercessions, and giving of thanks, be made for all men; For _____, and for all that are in _____; that _____ may lead a quiet and peaceable life in all _____ and _____."
Even here the Apostle Paul is including his own spiritual concerns in his prayers for the authorities. Do not forget to pray that the message of salvation might reach them also.

Summary:

We must converse with God with confidence, because He is our best Friend. It is important to maintain communion with God by talking with Him many times each day, because the believer can pray in any place and at any time. God wants to be adored and praised, but He wants to cleanse our hearts and lives so that what we say will be more than just words. The immediate confession of our sin is important so that nothing hinders our prayers. We should express our love, and thank God for all that He has done for us. We should pray to God with sincerity and faith, in the name of Jesus Christ. We should not be self-centered in our prayers, but also pray for others.

Suggestion: It is good to maintain a list of these people and their special requests for whom you should pray regularly.

Date	Names	Petition	Answered

REVIEW QUESTIONS

CHAPTER 9 — THE IMPORTANCE OF PRAYER

1. God wants to have communion with you. Why? _____

   _____

2. Besides our family, for whom should we pray?

   a. _____

   b. _____

   c. _____

   d. _____

   e. _____

   f. _____

3. Does God desire to hear the prayers of the sincere, unconverted sinner, who has a contrite and willing heart to repent of his sin, and to give himself to Christ? _____

4. Does God hear us for repeating our prayers loudly and frequently? _____

5. Where should we pray? _____

6. When should we pray? _____

7. How many times should we pray each day? _____

8. In all of our prayers, we should always pray that the _____ of God be done.

9. We should pray to _____ in the name of _____.

10. Just because we pray in the name of Jesus Christ, does it assure us that we will receive what we request? _____ Why? _____

11. Is it possible to make a wrong petition to God? _____ Why? (James 4:3)
_____

12. Some say, *prayer is an avenue where all can travel.* Is this true? ____ Why? _____ Please give a Bible verse to back it up.
_____

13. What three conditions does God require so that our prayers will be answered? (John 15:7, 16–17)

    1. _____

    2. _____

    3. _____

14. In 1 John 5:14–15, God tells us to pray according to His _____ and not according to our own desires.

15. Who helps us express our needs in prayer? _____

16. Give two reasons why it is important to pray every day. _____
_____

_____

17. For which things should we give thanks to God? _____
_____

18. Should we even give thanks for difficult things that happen to us? _____

19. Why should we worship God in prayer? _____

_____

20. Should we lift our hands into the air so that God can see our holy hands? _____ What does "lifting up holy hands, without wrath and doubting," signify? _____

_____

21. Prayer is one of the following things: *Please underline the correct answer:* (It is a religious rite), (It is something that is memorized), (It is an expression to God with our own words, which comes from the depth of our heart).

22. We talk to God through _____.

23. God talks to us through His _____.

———————◆▸❋◂◆———————

Please send your answers to the questions and any doubts that you might have regarding this lesson to the Bible Institute Correspondence Department:

philippi@becoming-a-christian.org

We all have many responsibilities before God. Study chapter 10 as we understand what God's Word instructs us to do.

— Chapter Ten —

The Responsibilities of the Believer

Now the God of peace, that brought again from the dead our Lord Jesus,
that great shepherd of the sheep, through the blood of the everlasting covenant,
make you perfect in every good work to do His will, working in you
that which is well pleasing in His sight, through Jesus Christ;
to whom be glory for ever and ever. Amen. Hebrews 13:20–21

We are a family and God is our father.

Ephesians 2:19 says, "Now therefore ye are no more strangers and foreigners,
but _____ with the saints, and of the _____ of
God." Now that we belong to Christ, we are members of the family of God, and
have many new privileges to enjoy. In addition to the new privileges, we have
responsibilities to assume. In obedience to the Word of God, it is necessary
to associate with those who are members of this spiritual family. Jesus Christ
wants us to be united in a group that the Bible calls *"The Local Church."*

I. God ordained the local church

1. What is a church? Our English word *church* comes from the Greek,
   ecclesia, or (*ek-kaleo= the called out ones*), which is translated *assem-
   bly or congregation*. At times it is translated, *called-out or separated
   ones*. What did Christ mean when He said, in Matthew 16:18, "I will
   build my church?" This is work that only Jesus Christ can do. Jesus
   Christ is the only one who can give us His faith and bring repentance
   for salvation. God has called us out of the world to follow Jesus Christ.

127

The Apostle John, in Revelation 21:2–3, makes reference to the Church as the bride of Christ: "And I John saw the holy city, new Jerusalem, coming down from God out of heaven, prepared as a _____ adorned for her husband. And I heard a great voice out of heaven saying, Behold, the tabernacle of _____ is with men, and he will dwell with them, and they shall be his people, and God himself shall be with them, and be their God."

2. Who is the head of the church? The Apostle Paul assures us, in Colossians 1:18, that Jesus Christ "is the head of the body, the church: who is the beginning, the firstborn from the dead; that in all things he might have the preeminence." We should not permit ourselves to be confused by those who ignore the fact that the *Body of Christ* is the *Church*, and the *Church* is the *Body of Christ*. We are members of His *Body*. When the Lord Jesus Christ comes again for His Church, it will not be some local church in particular, but for all truly born-again Christians. The Apostle Paul affirms this teaching in 1 Corinthians 12:12 saying: "For as the body is one, and hath many members, and all the members of that one body, being many, are one body: so also is Christ." Here it is not speaking of a local church.

3. When did Jesus begin to build His church? In the beginning of His ministry, Jesus Christ began to build His church. On the day of Pentecost, the Apostle Peter and the other apostles preached the salvation message of Jesus Christ, and 3,000 were converted to Christ, saved by God's grace, and baptized in water by immersion. We read this in Acts 2:41, "Then they that gladly received his word were baptized: and the same day there were added unto them about three thousand souls." The fact that there were *added unto them* (the *Body of Christ*), indicates that they were not the first. God called this group of real believers into one body, the *Church*. Throughout all the letters of the Apostles Paul, Peter, John and Matthew, as well as Luke and James, *the church of Jesus Christ* is mentioned. The word *church* appears more than one hundred times in the New Testament. The church of the New Testament is not the people of Israel of the Old Testament; however, Romans 4:1–9 affirms that Abraham and David were saved by faith, in the same way that we have been saved. Even though they were not part of the local church of Jesus Christ, they were by faith, part of the *Body of Christ*. As we look

back, by faith, to that supreme sacrifice of Jesus Christ for our sins on the cross, even so the believers of the Old Testament looked forward, by faith, to the supreme sacrifice of Jesus Christ for their sins, as the Lamb of God. We should not be confused thinking that true believers of the Old Testament will not participate in the rapture along with the believers of the New Testament. We are one *Body* in Christ Jesus.

4. What is a local church? A local church is a group of baptized believers (placed into the family of God, having repented with all their heart of their sin, and deposited their confidence in Jesus Christ as their sufficient Savior), united in the doctrine of Christ and the apostles, and committed to fulfill Christ's mandates and instructions. Then they are immersed in water identifying themselves with Christ and the local church. Read carefully the following passages: Matthew 28:18–20; Galatians 1:2,13,22; and Colossians 4:15–16. God uses the local church as an instrument in His hand to help us to grow daily in our spiritual life. We know very well that it is necessary to receive the right food in order to be healthy and grow physically. We should give the same importance to our spiritual nourishment that is able to help us grow and mature; otherwise the believer will be weak and sickly spiritually. The unity of true believers can only be the result of the work of Christ in our life. We need to maintain our testimony and union with Jesus Christ following the *sound doctrine* of the Word of God.

5. What things characterized the believers of the primitive church? Please read Acts 2:41–42, 47.

   a. They received the _____(the teachings).

   b. They were _____ (immersed in water).

   c. They continued in the _____ of the apostles.

   d. They continued in the _____one with other.

   e. They continued in the breaking of the _____.

   f. They continued in _____ (talking with God)

   g. They were _____ God (adoration).

II. The requirements to become a member of a local church

Each church is an independent entity, responsible to God for its own actions, government, and discipline. For this reason we find differences in practice, even some small differences in some doctrines between individual churches. For this reason it is very important to look for a church that will be faithful to the Word of God in its preaching and teaching. A good church must also teach separation from worldly practices and be faithful in practicing Biblical sound doctrine. To become a member of a local church, you must express your desire, request instruction and orientation from the pastor of that local church.

1. The conversion of the individual is crucial.

   It is a mandate from God that the person be converted, as it says in Acts 3:19: "_____ ye therefore, and be _____, that your sins may be blotted out, when the times of refreshing shall come from the presence of the Lord." It is important to maintain a good testimony and to show by your life that you belong to Christ and that you are truly His property. Please read Matthew 10:32; Luke 3:8; Romans 6:4.

2. The person must attend an orientation class.

   Most Bible-believing churches require a time before being baptized in order to give the new believer an opportunity to receive Biblical direction and instruction. This helps the new believer to understand more about Bible doctrine, and the principles and practices of the local church. It helps the new believer to know what the responsibilities will be as members of the church. It is important for the new believer to then be baptized biblically by immersion in water. Baptism is a mandate that Jesus Christ gave in Matthew 28:19–20. Through baptism we are publicly identifying ourselves with Jesus Christ and with the local church.

3. It is important to be in agreement with the teachings, principles and practices of the local church.

   God has ordained the pastor of the church to care for all the members and for those who attend. The Apostle Peter, in 1 Peter 5:2–3, affirmed this responsibility: "Feed the flock of God which is among you, taking the _____ thereof, not by constraint, but willingly; not for filthy lucre, but of a ready mind; Neither as being lords over God's heritage, but being _____ to the flock." It is necessary that they have a submissive attitude, as well as a desire to serve the Lord with all his heart. Hebrew 13:17 shows the importance of obeying the teaching and the discipline of the pastor of your church: "Obey them that have the rule over you, and _____ yourselves: for they watch for your _____, as they that must give _____, that they may do it with joy, and not with grief: for that is unprofitable for you."

III. The two ordinances of the local church

1. Baptism

a. Baptism is the immersion or submersion in water of the believer in obedience to the command of our Lord Jesus Christ, found in Matthew 28:19–20: "Go ye therefore, and teach all nations, _____ them in the name of the Father, and of the Son, and of the Holy Spirit: _____ them to observe all things whatsoever I have commanded you: and, lo, I am with you alway, even unto the end of the world."

b. When the believer is baptized by immersion in water, he is identified with Christ in His death, burial and resurrection. This act signifies what Christ did for us by taking our place in judgement in order to give us His salvation. Baptism, therefore, represents our death to sin, our burial or separation from the worldly things, and the resurrection to walk in a new life in Christ Jesus, and to serve Him with all our being. (Romans 6:5–6; Galatians 2:20)

c. Water baptism is our identification with the local church in their doctrine, principles and practices, projects and ministries. It is also a true identification with those who are members of that local body (the church). **By faith we are placed, or baptized into the family of God upon believing, (depositing our confidence) in Christ Jesus as our only, personal Savior.** Acts 2:38 proclaims, "Repent, and be _____ every one of you in the name of Jesus Christ for the _____ (forgiveness) of _____, and ye shall receive the gift of the Holy Spirit." This *gift* is salvation! **We must understand that this act has nothing to do with water.** The act of repenting of our sins is our own action. It is also our own decision to *put ourselves into* Christ Jesus, so that we become His property. In other words, we give ourselves totally to Christ Jesus for salvation, and Christ Jesus makes us members of His family. Peter again preached another message that was similar to the first, in Acts 3:19, when he gave emphasis to the same subject of salvation. He gave the order:

"Repent ye therefore, and be _____, that your sins may be blotted out, when the times of refreshing shall come from the presence of the Lord." The only way that sin can be forgiven, *blotted out*, is through a true conversion to Jesus Christ, being put (*baptized*) into Him. In other words, we give ourselves totally to Jesus Christ for salvation and He makes us a member of His family!

d. Baptism in water does not have any part in our salvation, nor does it give us special merits with God, nor can it help us to be more spiritual. It does not wash or take away our sins. Baptism in water is a clear testimony of our identification with Christ and the local church. But if the believer does not want to be baptized, it is an act of rebellion and is in direct disobedience to God. If you were already baptized once in obedience to Christ and His command, but the teachings of that church are in error, you are automatically associated with error. It is only right that you no longer remain associated with the baptism of a church that teaches error, but that you be baptized in water in a church that faithfully teaches and preaches sound doctrine and faithfully practices this teaching.

2. The Lord's Supper

a. The Lord's Supper is important for the Christian, because we are remembering the death and resurrection of our Lord Jesus Christ until He comes. In Luke 22:19 Jesus said that He was going to give His body to save those who deposit their confidence in Him: "And He took bread, and gave thanks, and brake it, and gave unto them, saying, This *(is)* my body which is given for you: this do in remembrance of me." Always we do it in remembrance of His physical death on the cross. By participating in this ordinance in **no way** are we again making a sacrifice of the body of Jesus Christ. **It is in memory of Him.**

b. Important questions regarding the elements

1) What does the bread without leaven mean? The bread without leaven (yeast) has an important meaning. It represents the person of Jesus Christ. In the Bible, *leaven* always symbolizes *corruption*, sin and error. Therefore in the Lord's Supper, bread <u>without yeast</u> is used to represent the Person of the Lord Jesus Christ in all His perfection.

2) What does the cup of grape juice, without fermentation, represent? The juice, made from grapes without fermentation, has an important meaning. It represents the blood of Jesus Christ. In the celebration of the Lord's Supper, grape juice without yeast or fermentation is always used because the fresh juice represents the perfection of Christ Jesus, not corruption, sin or error. The Apostle Paul, in 1 Corinthians 11:25, taught: "After the same manner also He took the cup, when He had supped, saying, this cup is the new testament in my blood: this do ye, as oft as ye drink it, in _____ of me."

c. Why should we participate in the Lord's Supper?

1) It is an order given by Jesus Christ in memory of Him. In no way can it bring us some special *grace* by participating. We partake of the Lord's Supper in obedience to His command.

2) We are recalling His horrible death on the cross, taking our terrible sins on Himself and paying what we deserve. We are remembering the peace and joy that we have with Christ and with the brethren. Jesus Christ began the Supper with His apostles in the upper room the night before His death. They did not eat His body neither did they drink His blood! Neither does the bread and juice now convert themselves into the body and blood of Jesus Christ. Those who promote such a teaching are blaspheming God. It is an immense error!

3) When we participate in the Lord's Supper, we are remembering that Jesus Christ will come again and the dead in Christ will be resurrected first, and immediately, we who are alive will be taken up with them. Paul stated in 1 Corinthians 11:26: "For as often as ye eat this bread, and drink this cup, ye do shew the Lord's death till He _____." This is the *blessed hope* of the Christian!

d. How often should we participate in the Lord's Supper? The Bible does not tell us how often we should receive the Lord's Supper, but it does state clearly in 1 Corinthians 11:26: "For as _____ as ye eat this bread, and drink this cup, ye do _____ the Lord's death till He come."

e. Is there a justified reason for not participating in the Lord's Supper? As a member of a local church, if there is unconfessed sin in your life, is it correct for you to partake of the Lord's Supper, if you have not confessed the sin that is your life? No! In 1 Corinthians 11:28–29 the Apostle Paul admonishes us to examine our hearts: "But let a man _____ himself, and so let him _____ of that bread, and _____ of that cup. For he that eateth and drinketh unworthily, eateth and drinketh damnation to himself, not discerning the Lord's body." We should examine ourselves in order to rectify with God the sin in our life, asking for forgiveness through Christ. Each one should examine his own heart, confess his sin to God, and ask for forgiveness. 1 John 1:9 teaches, "If we _____ our sins, he is faithful and just to _____ us our sins, and to _____ us from all unrighteousness." It tells us to get things right with the Lord **and then receive the elements.** Some believe that they cannot receive the elements because they do not deserve them, and they are not good enough to receive them. We obey God, not because we deserve His blessings, but because we love Him. Christ Jesus will never accept any excuse not to get our lives right with Him. Is there a justified reason for not partaking of the Lord's Supper? Yes! If you have recently been converted and have not yet become a member of a local church, then you should wait until you have become a member. However, you should be present, and pray and ask the Lord to forgive your sin and participate in that way. Do not let Satan rob you of your communion with God. Who is controlling your life? _____

IV. The responsibilities of the local church

The local church is a very important part of the Christian's life. There are those who have mistaken concepts regarding the local church and our responsibilities as believers. Some reject their God–given responsibilities and their commitment to Jesus Christ.

1. The meetings in the local church are <u>for the cultivation of spiritual growth of the members.</u> To be absent from these services in the church can only result in the impoverishment of the spiritual life of the Christian. Hebrew 10:23–26 gives important instructions for our spiritual growth: "Let us hold _____ the profession of our faith without

wavering; (for He is faithful that promised;) And let us _____
one another to provoke unto love and to good _____: Not _____
the assembling of ourselves together, as the manner of some is; but
_____ one another: and so much the more, as ye see the
day approaching. For if we _____ wilfully after that we have received the knowledge of the truth, there remaineth no more sacrifice for
sins." This admonishes us to be faithful in our church attendance. When
we lack this fidelity in church attendance, it is a serious sin. There is no
other remedy, but to repent and return to Christ to receive His pardon.
You must return to church with a changed attitude, determined to be
faithful to God and not to continue sinning against Him. The *day of the
Lord* belongs to Him, to worship Him and receive the teachings from
God's Word to be able to grow in the Lord and serve Him faithfully.

2. The local church has the responsibility <u>to preach all the council of
   the Word of God</u> on Sundays and during the week. The Apostle Paul
   gave the command, in 2 Timothy 4:1-3, to the pastors as follows: "I
   charge thee therefore before God, and the Lord Jesus Christ, who
   shall judge the quick and the dead at His appearing and His kingdom;
   _____ the _____; be instant in season, out of season _____,
   (in Greek it actually means – *to make a profound investigation*)
   _____, _____ with all longsuffering and _____.
   For the time will come when they will not endure sound doctrine; but
   after their own lusts (carnal desires) shall they heap to themselves
   teachers, having itching ears." (They will say what you want to hear.)
   The duty of the pastor and the teachers of the church is to obey what
   it says in Titus 2:1: "But _____ thou the things which become
   _____ doctrine." God will judge the pastor if he does not fulfill his
   ministry. In 2 Timothy 4:5, the Apostle Paul orders: "But watch thou
   in all things, endure afflictions, do the _____ of an evangelist, make
   full proof of thy ministry." We are reminded of the seriousness of being
   a pastor, in Hebrews 13:17: "They watch for your souls, as they that
   must give _____, that they may do it with joy, and not with grief:
   for that is unprofitable for you."

3. The local church has the obligation <u>to protect the members of the church
   from the attacks of error</u> and to prepare them to resist satanic forces.
   The Apostle Paul teaches, in Ephesians 6:10–18, that it is vital for us to

be prepared to combat the errors that Satan is always presenting. The verses 11–13 say: "Put on the _____ armour of _____, that ye may be able to _____ against the wiles of the _____. For we wrestle not against flesh and blood, but against principalities, against powers, against the rulers of the darkness of this world, against spiritual wickedness in high places. Wherefore take unto you the _____ armor of God, that ye may be able to withstand in the _____ day, (that is every day) and having done all, to _____." Satan wants to divide and discourage the brethren. The encouragement that we receive in the church through the teaching, the preaching of God's Word, and fellowship with the brethren in Christ, helps us to be prepared for the battle against false doctrine and Satan's attacks.

4. The local church has the responsibility <u>to prepare the new converts to be baptized</u>. It is the responsibility of the church to teach and to baptize those who are true disciples of Christ Jesus. Matthew 28:19 says, "Go ye therefore, and _____ all nations, baptizing them in the name of the Father, and of the Son, and of the Holy Spirit: _____ them to observe all things whatsoever I have commanded you: and, lo, I am with you alway, even unto the end of the world. Amen."

5. The local church has the responsibility <u>to serve the Lord's Supper</u> to the members of the church in obedience to the Word of God. The Apostle Paul shares in 1 Corinthians 11:26, what he had received from the Lord Jesus Christ: "For as often as ye eat this bread, and drink this cup, ye do shew the Lord's death till He come." Verse 24 commands: "Do this in _____ of me." We participate remembering what Christ has done for us.

6. The local church has the responsibility <u>to stimulate the members to pray together</u> for the church and its activities. We should pray especially for the workers of the church, the pastor, the deacons (servants of Christ) and the teachers. We should pray for the regular worship services. We should pray for the spiritual growth of the different phases of the work, their programs, and projects, including the Sunday School, youth group, missionaries, etc.

7. The local church has the obligation <u>to give responsibilities to faithful members of the church</u>. We are responsible before God to be good and **faithful administrators** of our life, our talents, our money, and our

time. 1 Corinthians 4:2 mentions: "it is _____ in stewards, that a man be found _____." God wants us to be faithful in everything.

The form of governing the local church is *Christocratic*, which signifies it is a democratic and congregational form of governing, of which Christ Jesus is the Head. The authority and the direction come from the Word of God by the Holy Spirit. The pastor is responsible to God and the church for what he is doing in fulfilling his responsibilities. In the primitive church, the apostles commissioned the members of the church with the responsibility of choosing spiritual men for the positions of the church. We see an example of this in Acts 6:1–7 where the order was given to, "Look ye out among you seven _____ of honest report, _____ of the Holy Spirit and wisdom, whom we may appoint over this business (work)."

The decisions on the activities and ministries of the local church are not made by a bishop, superintendent, president, or a convention, but by the members of the local church. The pastor directs the deacons (servants of the Lord) and the members in the determination of the matters, which concern the physical installation of the church. They all have equal privileges to voice their opinion, and they all vote in the meetings regarding those matters of the church. It is a privilege and a great responsibility to help in the decisions that affect the work of the Lord in the local church. However, touching the spiritual areas of doctrine and Biblical practice, there is no room for determining whether or not we will obey God's Word. We have no other option than to be completely directed by the Word of God. The authority and the leadership for the church come from the Word of God and the Holy Spirit. It is indispensable that each member study diligently the Bible and live in communion with God to be guided by the Holy Spirit in all the matters of his life, especially when it comes to participating in the ministry of the church.

8. To please God, it is important that the local church <u>maintain discipline and reverence in the services and meetings.</u> In 1 Corinthians 14:40 the Apostle Paul insisted: "Let all things be done decently and in _____." The discipline and order must be maintained in the personal life of the members in their work and homes. We should desire to have holiness in the church and in our life.

9. The local church has the responsibility to evangelize those who do not know the Lord Jesus Christ as their Savior. The church should have a visitation program with as many members as possible participating. Besides having organized visitation, each believer should give testimony to unsaved family members, neighbors, classmates, coworkers, and everywhere God gives us opportunity to evangelize. Peter gives us encouragement in 1 Peter 3:15, "But _____ the Lord God in your hearts (live holy lives for the Lord): and be ready always to _____ an answer to every man that asketh you a reason of the hope that is in you with meekness and fear."

Many church members are setting aside one hour each week to give a Bible class to an unsaved person, using the book, *Becoming a Christian*. These home Bible study classes are resulting in the salvation of many people, and are also a great spiritual encouragement to fellow believers. The Lord Jesus Christ gave the order in Matthew 28:19–20: "Go ye therefore, and teach all nations, baptizing them in the name of the Father, and of the Son, and of the Holy Ghost: Teaching them to observe all things whatsoever I have commanded you: and, lo, I am with you alway, even unto the end of the world. Amen." The ministry of making a disciple is not teaching a Christian more of God's Word; rather to bring an unsaved person through the teaching of God's Word to a saving relationship with Jesus Christ. Paul told us in Philippians 2:15 that we should: "be blameless and harmless, the sons of God, without rebuke, in the midst of a crooked and perverse nation, among whom ye shine as lights in the world." We have to maintain our devotion and obedience to Christ, and be faithful, and He will richly bless us.

10. The local church has the responsibility to provide a Bible orientation class to guide new believers in the basic Bible doctrines and to stimulate their spiritual growth.

11. The local church should not accept the worldly music styles of our day. What does *worldly* mean? Years ago Christians did not ask that question because they knew what was meant by the expression *worldly*. The entrance of *Christian contemporary music (CCM)* has brought great confusion into our churches. Many young people are asking their pastors, *Why do we only use old music that is boring and discouraging? Why can't we have the music that is popular and enjoyable? Why do*

*you call the music with repetitive rhythms **worldly** if it lifts the emotions and incites movement? Is it so bad to applaud with the beat?*

Worldliness simply means — *something of the world*, or *like the world*. In 2 Corinthians 4:4, Satan is called, "the god of this world." One of Satan's goals is to blind the minds and hearts of those who do not understand and receive the truth of the Gospel of Christ. Satan wants to introduce modern and *worldly* music into the church for the purpose of driving a wedge inside the church and causing a division among its members. *Worldly* music comes from a sinful life that provokes sensuality. The general practice is to put words that appear to be Christian to *worldly* music and then introduce it into the churches.

When prohibiting this type of music in the house that belongs to Christ Jesus, the reaction is as though something lovely and beautiful was being prohibited. The fact that contemporary music is popular does not make it right. The music that you desire reflects what you believe concerning God. If you are a true Christian, you should know that we have an all-powerful God, who wants to be adored and praised with reverent and majestic music. Ephesians 5:10 tell us that we should be, "Proving what is acceptable unto the Lord." Colossians 3:16 insists, "Let the word of Christ dwell in you richly in all wisdom; teaching and admonishing one another in psalms and hymns and spiritual songs, singing with grace in your hearts to the Lord."

Music is not amoral. Music has the power to influence you for good or for evil depending on its style and composition. Many of our generation deny the powerful influence of music. Some accept all types of music suggesting that it does not matter to God what types of music we listen to or use in our churches. Isaiah 5:20 declares: "Woe unto them that call evil good, and good evil; that put darkness for light, and light for darkness; that put bitter for sweet, and sweet for bitter!"

The Christian is to be different from the world, but not strange or odd. We should maintain a consecrated life to Christ, pleasing God the Father, because we belong to Him. In John 17:16–17, Jesus prayed for His followers in this way: "They are not of the world, even as I am not of the world. Sanctify them through thy truth: thy word is truth."

The Apostle Paul declared in 1 Corinthians 1:18, "For the preaching of the cross <u>is to them that perish foolishness</u>; but unto us which are saved it is the power of God." When a true believer separates himself to Christ, it "is to them that perish foolishness." The world rejects what the Bible says, but now modern Christendom tries to win the world through worldly music, with its contemporary rhythms and sensual styles. Of course, they want to call it, *Christian music*. Because of this fellowship, fusion or union with the world, there is confusion and a growing ignorance of the teachings of the Word of God regarding the believer's separation from physical, emotional and spiritual worldliness. God orders this separation in 2 Corinthians 6:14–18.

The Apostle Paul teaches the necessity of renouncing ungodliness and worldly desires in Titus 2:11–15: "For the grace of God that bringeth salvation hath appeared to all men, Teaching us that, denying ungodliness and worldly lusts, we should live soberly, righteously, and godly, in this present world; Looking for that blessed hope, and the glorious appearing of the great God and our Savior Jesus Christ; Who gave himself for us, that he might redeem us from all iniquity, and purify unto himself a peculiar people, zealous of good works. These things speak, and exhort, and rebuke with all authority. Let no man despise thee." We should not let the scorn of the world affect us.

Paul warns in Titus 3:8–11: "This is a faithful saying, and these things I will that thou affirm constantly, that they which have believed in God might be careful to maintain good works. These things are good and profitable unto men. But avoid foolish questions, and genealogies, and contentions, and strivings about the law; for they are unprofitable and vain. A man that is an heretick (**causes division**) after the first and second admonition reject; knowing that he that is such is subverted, and sinneth, being condemned of himself."

We should not endorse *worldly* music in the church of the Lord Jesus Christ nor in the homes of the Christian, because it will cause a great division in the true Church of Christ. Jude 1:3–4 gives this warning: "Beloved, when I gave all diligence to write unto you of the common salvation, it was needful for me to write unto you, and exhort you that ye should earnestly contend for the faith which was once delivered unto the saints. For there are certain men crept in unawares, who were before of old ordained to this condemnation, ungodly men, turning the grace of our God into lasciviousness, and denying the only Lord God, and our Lord Jesus Christ."

V. The responsibilities of the members of the local church

Each member is important in the function of a local church. We have to remember that we are supporting the purposes of the local church in all its functions. We should consider these purposes as our personal responsibility.

1. Each member of the local church should faithfully attend all the meetings of the church to hear the teaching and counsel of the Word of God on Sunday and during the week. We should not miss any of the Bible studies or services, because we must desire to grow in the knowledge of the Word of God to be able to help others also.

2. It is the responsibility of each member of the local church to look after the other members and to protect them against the attacks of error, and encourage them to combat against the satanic forces in a united manner. Have we shown concern about the members and visitors who are not faithfully attending? It is necessary to visit them when they are sick or experiencing discouraging times. One of the personal responsibilities of the members of the local church is to cultivate spiritual growth among the brethren. We have to encourage them to be obedient to the Word of God.

3. It is indispensable for the members to keep peace and unity among the brethren. If some conflict exists among the brethren it has to be resolved. In Matthew 5:23–24, Christ cautioned the believers: "Therefore if thou bring thy _____ to the altar, and there rememberest that thy brother hath ought against thee; _____ there thy _____ before the altar, and go thy way; first be _____ to thy brother, and then come and _____ thy gift." Here it speaks of the offering that we present to God. It is not making reference to the Lord's Supper. Besides being the offering for the support of the ministry, it is making reference to us, as it says in Roman 12:1: "I beseech you therefore, brethren, by the mercies of God, that ye present your _____ a living sacrifice, holy, acceptable unto God, which is your reasonable service." We should do this every day. We have to solve these conflicts as soon as possible.

4. All the members should pray in a united way for the church, their leaders and the activities. We should set aside time every day for individual and family devotions to read the Bible and pray. In 2 Thessalonians 3:1 the

Apostle Paul requests, "Finally, brethren, pray for us, that the word of the Lord may have free _____, and be glorified, even as it is with you."

5. All the members should participate in the support of the church with their tithes and offerings. When we are faithful to Christ, and fulfill the responsibility of giving our tithes to God, we are participating in the support of the work and the ministries of the church. The ministry of the church is the pastor's support, the promotion of missions, the support of missionaries and evangelism in general. The only way to maintain these ministries is with the tithes and offerings of brethren. Jesus said in Mark 12:17, "Render to Caesar the things that are Caesar's, and to God the things that are God's." With joy in our heart, we should give our tithe and offering to God as He has prospered us every week. The Apostle Paul, in 2 Corinthians 9:5–8, gave the following admonition: "Every man according as he _____ in his heart, so let him give; not grudgingly, or of necessity: for God loveth a _____ giver." It is a example of love according to Matthew 6:21: "For where your treasure is, there will your _____ be also." God does not want us to be thieves, as mentioned in Malachi 3:8; "Will a man _____ God? Yet ye have robbed me. But ye say, Wherein have we robbed thee? In tithes and offerings." The solution is in Malachi 3:10; "Bring ye all the tithes into the storehouse, that there may be meat in mine house, and prove me now herewith, saith the Lord of hosts, if I will not open you the windows of heaven, and pour you out a blessing, that there shall not be room enough to receive it." In this passage, God is not promising material wealth for us, but His rich blessings and provisions for our necessities.

As faithful Christians, we should have a systematic way of tithing and giving as the Apostle Paul in 1 Corinthians 16:2: "Upon the first day of the week let every one of you lay by him in store, as God hath prospered him, that there be no gatherings when I come." It requires discipline to set aside our tithe as an act of worship and love for Christ. We have to remember that it is our church, and it is our responsibility to care for it and to support its physical and spiritual growth.

6. All the members of the local church should accept responsibilities and positions, and faithfully carry out that ministry. It is important for the

progress of the work of Christ. We should ask God for opportunities to serve Him in the local church. 1 Peter 4:10 says, "As every man hath received the _____, even so _____ the same one to another, as good stewards of the manifold grace of God."

7. All the members of the local church have the privilege to evangelize with the Word of God. All Christians should teach someone new the Word of God, take them to church and win them for Christ. Christ Jesus commands us in Mark 16:15, "Go ye into all the world, and preach the gospel to every creature." The ministry of making disciples is not only the act of teaching someone, but to bring them to a true conversion to Christ.

8. Besides reaching souls for Christ, we have to disciple the new ones and to encourage them in the needs and problems of their spiritual life. The Apostle Paul admonishes us in 2 Timothy 2:1–2: "Thou therefore, my son, be _____ in the grace that is in Christ Jesus. And the things that thou hast heard of me among many witnesses, the same commit thou to _____ men, who shall be able to teach others also." Using this book as a guide, is a good way to evangelize and disciple others in the home or in classes in the church.

VI. What is the "blessed hope" of the Christian?

1. Christ Jesus will come again for us! With clarity Paul teaches us in 1 Thessalonians 4:13–18, and John 14:1–3, about this glorious event of the coming of Christ Jesus in the air, when He will take us to be with Him. Many times reference is made to this great event as the *rapture of the believer*.

2. What happens when the believer dies? Their soul and spirit go immediately to be with Christ. The Apostle Paul teaches in 2 Corinthians 5:6–8: "Therefore we are always confident, knowing that, whilst we are at home in the _____, we are _____ from the Lord: (For we walk by faith, not by sight:) We are confident, I say, and willing rather to be absent from the body, and to be present with the Lord." The body goes to the sepulcher while waiting for the physical resurrection. 1 Corinthians 15:51–53 explains about the change that will happen to the our body: "Behold, I shew you a mystery; We shall not all sleep, but we shall all be changed, in a moment, in the twinkling of an eye, at

143

the last trump: for the trumpet shall sound, and the dead shall be raised incorruptible, and we shall be _____. For this corruptible must put on incorruption, and this mortal must put on immortality." We will have a body transformed with the same qualities as the body of our Lord Jesus Christ when He arose from the dead; however, each individual will have his own characteristics as they were known here on the earth. This is the wonderful hope of each true Christian. The following passages confirm this blessed hope of the Christian: 1 John 3:1–3; Jude 1: 24–25 and Colossians 1:21–29. I want to see you there in heaven with Christ!

Student

I trust that the study of God's Word has been a blessing, and that this book has been a useful guide. The principal purpose of this book is to evangelize those who do not know the Lord Jesus Christ as their Savior. If this book has been used by God to help you give your life to Christ, to God be the honor and the glory. I would love to hear from you and have you share your testimony with me, so that I can pray for you!

If you have doubts or questions, please write to us. Be sure to send us your complete address. Please elaborate your question as clearly as possible. This will help us give you the adequate answer.

"And the very God of peace sanctify you wholly;
and I pray God your whole spirit and soul and body be preserved
blameless unto the coming of our Lord Jesus Christ.
Faithful is He that calleth you, who also will do it."
1 Thessalonians 5:23–24

May God richly bless you!

Myron L. Philippi

Pastor Myron L. Philippi

Chapter 1. (Page 7)

1. No. It is not according to the Bible.
2. No. Many pretend, but are not.
3. No. Jesus said that He never knew them.
4. No. The Bible tells us how to have this security.
5. No. It is contrary to the Bible.
6. Yes. The Bible tells us how to have this security.
7. Yes. The Bible tells us how to be saved.
8. No. Ephesians 2:8-9
9. No. Ephesians 2:8-9
10. No. Ephesians 2:8-9
11. No. Ephesians 2:8-9
12. No. Matthew 7:21-23
13. No. Galatians 2:16
14. No. There are many gods in this world.
15. No. Ephesians 2:8-9
16. Yes. He was taught by Gamaliel. Acts 22:3
17. No. He persecuted the Christians.
18. Yes. He was very religious.
19. No. Titus 3:5
20. Yes. He repented of his sin and put his full confidence in Christ.
21. No. He was extremely sad when he went to Damascus.
22. No. Experiences cannot save us.
23. No. James 2:19
24. No. Many things can cause changes in a life.
25. No. John 10:27 – We hear God's word and faithfully follow Jesus Christ.

Chapter 2. (Page 24)

1. Sin
2. No
3. All have disobeyed Him
4. No. Christ came for those who realize they are lost.
5. Yes. We must first realize our sinful condition.
6. Yes. This is how God sees us.
7. Repent of our sin.
8. No. God never will violate our personal desires.
9. No. Ephesians 2:8-9
10. No
11. No.
12. No. We are all sinners. Romans 3:23
13. False
14. True
15. False
16. True
17. True
18. False
19. True
20. Jesus Christ – God
21. Jesus Christ
22. Jesus Christ

Chapter 3. (Page 31)

1. Yes
2. Yes
3. No
4. Yes
5. Yes
6. No
7. No
8. Yes
9. Yes
10. No
11. Yes, Yes

Chapter 4. (Page 41)

1. False
2. False
3. True
4. True
5. True
6. True
7. False
8. True
9. False
10. True
11. True

12. True
13. True
14. False
15. True
16. True

Chapter 5. (Page 61)

1. To have eternal life. For fellowship with God.
2. Dying on the cross to save us.
3. By faith
4. Yes
5. No
6. Yes

Chapter 6. (Page 81)

1. To reconcile us to God. To forgive our sin and take it away.
2. This is for you to answer.
3. God's Word gives us complete assurance.
4. 2 Timothy 1:12 + many more.
5. Yes, I am a member of the Family of God.
6. Those who are separated from the world for the use of God. True born again Christians.
7. Once, all
8. Yes
9. Nothing
10. Nothing
11. Sin
12. None
13. No
14. No, none
15. Only one time
16. No, External things cannot bring God's grace or help.
17. God required it in the Old Testament.
18. Confess our sin, and forsake them.
19. He will give an account of himself to God for good and bad. To bring us back into fellowship with Him.
20. Jesus Christ, God's family.

21. I will give them eternal life.
22. "No one is able to take them out of my Father's hand."
23. Yes, good and bad, No

Chapter 7. (Page 100)

1. Bible
2. No one
3. Yes, We are combating the world, flesh and devil.
4. Love, joy, peace, patience, gentleness, goodness,
5. World, Flesh, Devil
6. Faithful, suffer, escape, bear.
7. Prayer and Bible study
8. The spiritual battle never ends.
9. We belong only to the Lord Jesus Christ and we should be faithful to represent Him.
10. Those practices are not Biblical and are in opposition to God.
11. The Holy Spirit
12. –Is this activity necessary?
   –Is it a help in my spiritual life, or for the spirituality of others?
   –Is this thing or activity controlling me?
   –What would Christ do?
   –Being involved in this activity or possessing this thing, am I giving a good testimony of Christ Jesus to those who see me?
13. Ask God for help, submit to Him, be prepared, put on the armor of God's Word, watch and pray, resist the devil, hide God's Word in our heart, repent of our sins.

Chapter 8. (Page 111)

1. The Holy Spirit.
2. 40
3. The Law or the Pentateuch The History of Israel
   The Poems, The Prophets
4. The History of Christ, History of

the Primitive Church, Doctrine, Prophecy
5. Doctrine,
Reproof,
Correction,
Instruction,
Maturity
6. Hear the Word.
Read the Word.
Study the Word.
Meditate on the Word
Memorize the Word
Obey the Word

20. No. It is speaking symbolically to help us realize that God sees the sin that we have committed. God insists that we recognize the sin in our life, repent, and that we confess it to Him.
21. It is an expression to God with our own words, which come from the depth of our heart.
22. Prayer
23. Word

Chapter 9. (Page 124)

1. We belong to Jesus Christ, He loves us, we love Him.
2. a. For ourselves, family and friends,
b. For believers and for unbelievers,
c. For brethren in the faith.
d. For the sick,
e. For ministers,
f. For government authorities
3. Yes
4. No
5. Everywhere, anywhere
6. Anytime
7. Many
8. Will
9. God the Father, – Jesus Christ
10. No, It is not a secret password.
11. Yes, Because of wrong attitudes, wrong desires, wrong intentions.
12. No, We only pray to the Father and Jesus Christ.
13. I need to abide in Christ, God's Word must abide in me, – I must obey His Word.
14. Will
15. The Holy Spirit
16. To maintain fellowship with God, and maintain a clean life.
17. Everything, the good and bad
18. Yes, It is God's will.
19. It is part of worship that He desires and deserves.